The Writers' Compound

The Story of Four American Authors in
Key West

The Writers' Compound

The Story of Four American Authors in Key West

By Jack L. Roberts

Designed by Michael Owens

FOREWORD BY JUDITH DAYKIN

PALM TREE PRESS

Palm Springs, CA

Palm Tree Press
519 Jade Lane
Palm Springs, CA 92264

Photo Credits: We have made every effort to trace and contact copyright holders for the photographs that appear in this book. If an error or omission is brought to our attention, we will be pleased to make the appropriate correction in future printings of the book. Unless otherwise noted, photos are public domain. Page 11: Hemingway and Passos: Ernest Hemingway Collection. John F. Kenney Presidential Library and Museum, Boston; Page 55: John Hersey: Photo: Alison Shaw; Page 73: Richard Wilbur: Photo courtesy of Arlo Haskell, The Key West Literary Seminar; Page 76: Photo of Richard and Charlee Wilbur. (wedding) Daily Hampshire Gazette; Page 80: Photo of Wilbur and Charlee Wilbur: Merrill, James, "Richard & Charlee Wilbur," *WUSTL Digital Gateway Image Collections & Exhibitions*, Washington University Libraries, Department of Special Collections. Page 84: Photo: Courtesy of Judith Daykin.

Library of Congress Control Number: 2018910491

First Printing: December 2018

ISBN-10: 0692184856

ISBN-13: 978-0692184851

Printed in the USA

DEDICATION

In memory of my friend and longtime compound resident
Richard (Dick) Reynolds.

Key West is "mysterious, funky, and indescribably exotic."

James Leo Herlihy, author of Midnight Cowboy

"It [is] very much like a cloud full of Cuban senoritas, coconut palms, and waiters carrying ice water. The place is a paradise."

Wallace Stevens, Poet

Key West is an island of "extraordinary charm."

Richard Wilbur, Poet

The Writers' Compound, Old Town, Key West

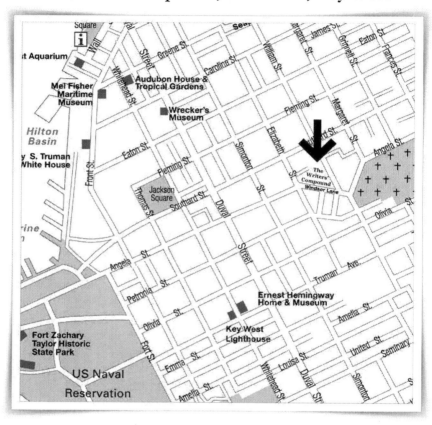

TABLE OF CONTENTS

FOREWORD

IN HIS BOOK, *The Writers' Compound*, Jack Roberts has captured the essence of writing and writers in Key West, Florida. Key West is known for many things, but its long-standing appeal to the writing community was and IS a given.

I guess we (my partner John Price and I) were closest to the Wilburs and the Herseys, as those things go. The Ellisons were almost never here in 1984, when we bought into the compound. And John and Judith Ciardi were around at the holidays, but not always through "season" in the winters. As "theater people," John and I felt a compatibility with the writers in the compound – an affinity for slightly eccentric, open, frank "artists" with whom we were comfortable and at ease. I think that's why Key West was so welcoming to writers, and why the writers felt they were "home" when they were here.

It was a lovely co-existence. In the early days, I was still working in New York City—first at the Brooklyn Academy of Music and later running City Center. We felt a sense of "honor" to share the company of these folks—our friends in Key West, with their reputations and awards and lofty accomplishments. Dick Wilbur had a working knowledge of our theater projects and always seemed interested in hearing the latest Broadway gossip, which we were happy to pass along!

The feeling I got from this book was of nostalgia, of fond memories, cocktail parties on the pool deck, of the fragrant smells and the breeze and the joy of being here in this small town with the most interesting, entertaining, smart, clever, inspiring fellow citizens, especially those who lived with us in the Writers' Compound on Windsor Lane! It's tempting to bring on the clichés— "those were the days" —but living here in those years was different than living here now. The "small-town," secluded aspect of Key West really has gone the way of all good ideas at this point. Development, tourism, the pressures of growth and change have impacted the infinite and intimate nature of a small community such as ours and changed the dynamic – and not necessarily for the better.

That's why this book is such a critical snapshot of these four incredible writers, their similarities and their differences, how they fit into the fabric of the social and intellectual personality of this little town, and how their presence influenced and impacted it – and its stature among writers everywhere.

This book will be a touchstone not only to writers but also to anyone else interested in the history of a community that nurtured and encouraged its artists – painters, sculptors, actors, and creative people of all stripes. Key West has always attracted this rare element of society – starting with our pirates, then staying in the Union during the Civil War when the rest of the State of Florida joined the Confederacy. And I DO believe this continues today. I know that I treasure the population of smart, interesting and curious residents who provide Key West with its heart and soul, and I hope you will find that spirit of adventure and creativity in Jack Roberts' book! I know I did! A joyful stepping back in time to relish the idea which was the Writers' Compound.

— Judith Daykin
Compound Resident
Founder, New York City Center's
Encores! Great American Musicals in Concert

PROLOGUE

IN 2010, I HAD THE OPPORTUNITY to live in one of the most famous residential locations in Key West—a one-acre secluded area in the center of Old Town with eleven small homes—a tropical oasis widely and affectionately known as The Writers' Compound.

Starting in 1976, the compound had been the winter retreat for four contemporary American writers—two poets and two novelists; three white and one black; two Pulitzer Prize winners and a National Book Award winner.

I occupied a small, one-room studio in the center of this exotic paradise, a veritable botanical garden with beautiful lush ficus trees, ginger blooms, and majestic travelers' palms—those palm tree imposters related to banana trees.

"You know your studio used to be the writing studio for John Hersey," my friend and landlord, Dick Reynolds, told me on the day I moved in. I acknowledged as much, vaguely having remembered reading *A Bell for Adano*, Hersey's Pulitzer Prize–winning novel, somewhere along the line.

I had known Dick casually for more than thirty years, having first met him when we both owned homes in Sag Harbor, Long Island, NY, but had lost touch after I had moved to California in 1997.

Dick was a rotund, soft-spoken gentleman of the old school of gentlemen—the nicest man anyone could ever know—who was so articulate and spoke with such precision that no matter what he said, you were convinced it was of the utmost importance. I loved listening to him. He was as much a philologist as his more scholarly neighbors and could recount the tiniest detail of the day as if he were recounting the pomp and pageantry of a coronation.

He would scuff around the compound or down Windsor Lane to his beat-up old Mercedes in orange Crocs, which I was sure would one day cause him to trip and kill himself.

One night we decided to go to one of his favorite Key West restaurants for dessert—The Flaming Buoy Filet Co. on Packer. As we walked down Windsor Lane (truth be told, he scuffed), across Truman to Packer where "chocolate-chocolate chip Belgian waffles" awaited (an amazing dessert at The Flaming Buoy), we talked about my career in educational publishing.

Dick knew that I had been a longtime editor and writer of educational materials for elementary and middle school students and their teachers, first at Children's Television Workshop (now Sesame Workshop) and later at Scholastic Inc., an internationally known educational publishing company. I was also the author of many nonfiction books (mostly biographies) for young readers. I mentioned to Dick that night that I was trying to decide who or what to write about next.

"Rather than write another book for kids," I remember him saying, "why don't you write about the four writers who lived in the compound? There are many people here in the compound and in Key West who knew them at that time and would probably have great stories to tell."

Then, he added, "Since you're living in John Hersey's writing studio, the vibes should be quite wonderful from the get-go." And so, they were.

It was with that simple suggestion that I immediately set to work researching the lives of these writers—John Ciardi, poet, etymologist, and translator of Dante's *Inferno*; Ralph Ellison, author of *Invisible Man*; Richard Wilbur, U.S. poet laureate and winner of the Pulitzer Prize for Poetry twice in his career; and John Hersey, winner of the Pulitzer Prize for Fiction for *A Bell for Adano*, in 1945, and author of the definitive story of World War II, *Hiroshima*, a journalistic masterpiece that tells the powerful and compassionate story of what happened on August 6, 1945 when the United States dropped the first atomic bomb on a city.

I soon discovered while the histories of each of these gentlemen were very different—Ciardi born to a poor Italian family in Massachusetts, Ellison born to a poor black Oklahoma family, Hersey born to an American missionary family in China, and Wilbur born to a middle-class family, both artistic and literary, in New Jersey—they were very much alike in one key aspect: they all achieved early success in the literary field—Ciardi with the publication of his first book of poems *Homeward to America* in 1940 when he was twenty-four years old; Wilbur with the publication of his first book *The Beautiful Changes and Other Poems* in 1947 at the age of twenty-six; Hersey who won the Pulitzer Prize in 1945 for his novel *A Bell for Adano* when he was thirty; and Ellison, the "late bloomer" in the group, who won the National Book Award for Fiction for *Invisible Man* in 1953 at the age of thirty-nine.

DURING THE NEXT SIX MONTHS as I began my research, current residents of the compound who had known these men and their wives, as well as other Key West writers, publishers, and agents, graciously gave their time for extensive interviews. It was clear from these interviews that there was a fascinating story to be told about these four remarkable writers.

My first interview was with my friend, landlord, and now mentor, Dick Reynolds. We sat at his big round kitchen table in front of double-wide French doors opened to a lush patio, the table cluttered with magazines, newspapers, books, and a hobbit's assortment of mathoms that never seemed to find their way into a bottom drawer or the back of a closet or better yet the trash. Yet, somehow the Command Center functioned efficiently for everything important in Dick's life, and I returned there frequently to discuss with Dick the various interviews I had and to get clarity on dates and people, places, and things.

But, then, as often happens in life, my particular path took another turn, and I returned to my home in Palm Springs, California. As a result, I put the Writers' Compound project aside. Instead, I spent the next several years launching and growing Curious Kids Press, an educational publishing company focused primarily on books about countries and cultures around the world for young readers

Then, one morning in late September 2017, I was scrolling through my emails when I saw one from another Key West friend and compound resident, Judith Daykin, who had also encouraged me along with Dick to write about the compound. She was writing to give me an update about Hurricane Irma that had passed over Key West a couple of weeks earlier, a Category 4 hurricane, the most powerful hurricane to strike the Florida Keys in more than half a century. She told me that all the homes in the compound were safe, "though the remaining ficus trees go down when someone sneezes," she said. She ended her email with: "Have you thought more about your book about the compound? We all wish you would think about finishing it."

That simple request was the impetus for the resurrection of the project. I reread the transcripts of the hours of taped interviews I had conducted years earlier and vowed to complete the story I had wanted to tell for almost a decade.

The result is this admittedly slim volume which offers a "slice of life," as it were—a rather arbitrary sequence of events and anecdotes—of four American writers and their interactions with one another during a short period of time in a specific location toward the last quarter or so of their lives.

It is not intended as a critique of their work, nor as a full biography of each author. (Both critique and biography have been accomplished successfully over the years by many others.)

Rather, it is an attempt to capture the temperament, imagination, and character of these men and the literary environment within which they resided for several months each year.

The book includes an introduction to Key West from its founding in 1822 and relates how the island evolved into a place for writers—a place, according to Key West author James (Jimmy) Kirkwood, winner of the Tony Award and the Pulitzer Prize for Drama for the Broadway musical *A Chorus Line*, where "all the fascinating and crazy people" live. "And I don't use the word 'crazy' pejoratively," he added.

THIS BOOK IS A WORK OF CREATIVE NONFICTION, and though some liberties have been taken with dialogue and detail, in all important aspects, the information in scenes is based on known facts. As John Berendt concedes in his introduction to *Midnight in the Garden of Good and Evil*, "Where the narrative strays from strict nonfiction, my intention has been to remain faithful to the characters and to the essential drift of events as they really happened." I agree.

The acknowledged "godfather" of creative nonfiction, Lee Gutkind, explains the genre this way. "The general tenet of creative nonfiction is that the writer is permitted and encouraged to use the techniques of the fiction writer in order to communicate facts and ideas." Gutkind summarized the essence of creative nonfiction as "true stories well told."

I hope that's what I have accomplished.

Pulitzer Prize-winning novelist Alison Lurie once said to me, "Writing nonfiction is a lot harder than writing fiction." (She has done both.) "With fiction, if you say, 'It was a dark and stormy night,' no one is going to question it. But with nonfiction, if you make that claim, you had better be sure it really was a dark and stormy night on the night in question."

She is quite right, of course. And while I have tried diligently to live up to Lurie's admonition regarding facts and details, and while I have benefited greatly from the memories and recollections of many people, any errors in fact in this book are entirely mine.

ACKNOWLEDGMENTS

WRITING THIS BOOK has taken me on an amazing adventure—not only into the lives of four fascinating contemporary American authors, but into the rich history of an island paradise and its community of writers.

But, of course, I couldn't have made this journey into the past without the help and encouragement of many people. Their stories and anecdotes about Key West and about the four gentlemen who are the subject of this book have enriched the narrative immeasurably. At the same time, their critique of the manuscript and suggestions for improvements (as well as corrections) have had a profound beneficial impact on this book. For their help, I am enormously grateful and wish specifically to thank the following individuals.

First, I must thank Judith Daykin who not only encouraged me to write this book long ago, but then waited patiently for me to do so. Judith's gentle nudging (over seven years) finally got me going and her constant encouragement kept me going. Thank you.

Charles Lee, Billy Cauthen, and Richard (Dick) Reynolds (deceased) are three men for whom I will always be in their debt. They provided intimate details of the four writers who lived in the compound, as well as their knowledge of the history of the compound and of Key West during the last three decades of the twentieth century, as did Tom Wilson and Ed Block. Thank you, thank you, thank you.

An enormous expression of gratitude goes to Pulitzer Prize

winner Alison Lurie, author Edward Hower, poet David Wojahn, and publisher Ross Claiborne. My interviews with these individuals were not only enlightening, but thoroughly entertaining.

I also need to thank a group of people who have never been to Key West, so were experiencing the island for the first time from my perspective. They include Elizabeth (Jerry) Edelen, Tricia Ross, David Norton, and Roselle Hernandez. Their insightful questions and criticisms guided me in further research and reconfirmation of facts.

Tony Award winner and friend Donna McKechnie shared her fond recollections of James Kirkwood, and at the same time helped to provide greater context for the Key West of the 1970s.

A special thank-you goes to Key West real estate agent Gary Thomas (*info@preferredpropertieskeywest.com*) who graciously provided photos of the compound (including the one on the cover) without asking for anything in return. Nevertheless, in return, I extend my grateful appreciation. And, of course, no book about Key West could be written without the help of Tom Hambright, manager of the Key West archives, Key West Public Library. No matter what you need to know or research about Key West, Tom is the man to go to.

I also want to thank my friend Tony Maietta, co-author of *The Marble Faun of Grey Gardens*, a beautifully written 2018 memoir and a behind-the-scenes look at the story of Mrs. Edith Bouvier Beale and her daughter "Little Edie" of East Hampton. I had the enormous benefit of talking with Tony at length about creative nonfiction and the importance of adhering to facts while at the same time creating a compelling story. Thank you, my friend.

Finally, I want to thank Michael Owens, my partner of thirty-six years, without whom this journey would not have been possible, nor, more importantly, worthwhile. He graciously read and reread every draft tirelessly, even on those days when I know he would have much rather been watching tennis. His constructive suggestions were always spot on. I am paraphrasing poet Richard Wilbur when I say I am so very lucky that years ago Michael decided I would do.

INTRODUCTION

THE END OF THE ROAD

"The soul of Key West is made up of the characters
who blazed the trail to the end of the road. We only
follow in their wake."

-- Singer/Songwriter Jimmy Buffett

Introduction

THE END OF THE ROAD

IN 1984, A YOUNG MAN named Billy Cauthen fled a tumultuous, drug-fueled relationship in Tampa, Florida, for what singer-songwriter Jimmy Buffett has called "the end of the road" —a tropical island 160 miles southwest of Miami and the southernmost part of the continental United States— a town that James Leo Herlihy, author of *Midnight Cowboy*, once described as "mysterious, funky, and indescribably exotic." That place is Key West.

Cauthen wasn't the first disenchanted and heartbroken nomad from the mainland to speed down the 113-mile Overseas Highway to Key West with the hope of escaping a bad situation or chasing a new adventure. From its earliest days, Key West was a magnet for an amalgam of "world wanderers from every portion of the globe, brought to Key West by chance or inclination, and held here by her lotus charms."

As Cauthen crossed over the Cow Key Channel bridge from Stock Island to Key West for the last leg of his trip, he must have thought about how in some ways Key West was a renegade from the mainland like himself. Only two years earlier, in fact, Key West had humorously "seceded" from the Union and formed the tongue-in-cheek Conch (pronounced konk) Republic with the apropos motto: "We Seceded Where Others Failed."

While the secession was humorous, the motivation was

real. The U.S. government had set up a Border Patrol roadblock and checkpoint on U.S. 1, just north of Florida City. Vehicles to and from Key West were being stopped and searched for narcotics and illegal immigrants, which caused disruption of tourist traffic to and from Key West. The mayor and city council of Key West argued at the time that be setting up the equivalent of a border station, the government was treating Key West as if it were a foreign nation. So, they reasoned, they might as well become one. (They declared war on the U.S. one day, surrendered after one minute, and then applied for a billion dollars in foreign aid.)

As the sensuous sea breeze competed with Tina Turner's hit song "What's Love Got to Do with It," the Queen of Rock 'n' Roll's 1984 iconic anthem to emotional survival and to relationships gone bad, Cauthen's great escape headed into the home stretch where U.S. 1 continues west, first as North Roosevelt Boulevard and then Truman Avenue to the intersection of Truman and Whitehead Street. There, he would turn right and proceed a few more blocks to the Monroe County courthouse at the intersection of Whitehead and Fleming—his final destination—Mile Marker Zero.

ONE HUNDRED AND SIXTY-TWO years earlier on January 19, 1822, John W. Simonton—a member of a prominent mercantile family in Mobile, Alabama—had purchased this spit of land, then called Cayo Hueso (or "bone island") from Juan Pablo Salas. Salas had acquired the island several years before that in a land grant from the Spanish governor of Florida "in consideration of several services rendered by him at different times."

Simonton had met Salas on a trip to Havana and was immediately intrigued by the business opportunity Salas presented to him. As a savvy opportunist, Simonton was aware of the island's potential economic opportunities, given its deep-water port—the deepest port between New Orleans, LA and Norfolk, VA—the island's strategic location (certain to be an appealing location to the U.S. Navy in the future), and its likely acquisition by the United States. (Florida had already been ceded to the U.S. a year earlier.)

As a businessman, Simonton had always been guided by one principle: "Capital and capitalists will go where profit is to be found."

So, on January 19, 1822, in what clearly was a prescient business decision, Simonton purchased the tiny island, measuring four miles (6.4 km) long and 1.5 miles (2.4 km) wide, for the grand sum of $2,000.00 (approximately $40,000 in 2018). And sure enough, two months later, on March 30, 1822, Lieutenant M.C. Perry, commander of the United States schooner *Shark*, planted the U.S. flag in Key West, ordered a seventeen-gun salute, and claimed the Keys as United States property. That set the obscure island—once considered by the Spanish to be North Havana—on a trajectory that within a very few short years would make Key West the richest city per capita in the United States, thanks in large part to both the thriving sponge market (Key West sponges were considered better than those brought in from the Gulf Coast) and the salvage industry, brought about in the early 1800s when commercial vessels would crash on the coral reef that surrounds the island.

In the early part of the century that followed, Henry Flagler, a railroad tycoon and cofounder of Standard Oil, opened the gateway to paradise and debauchery with his Over-Seas Railroad, 156 miles of railroad track—mostly over water—from Miami to Key West, a project that the best engineers at the time said couldn't be done and which later, when it was done, was hailed as the Eighth Wonder of the World. Flagler simply called it a "dream fulfilled."

At the same time, Flagler also conceived the Casa Marina, a

luxury hotel on the southern edge of the island with one of the few sand beaches in Key West, which opened on New Year's Eve 1920. Although Flagler died before the hotel's construction began in 1918, it was intended from the start to accommodate wealthy customers arriving in Key West on Flagler's Overseas Railroad, often as a stopover on their way to Havana, traveling either by island ferries or later by Pan American Airlines.

A visit by President Warren G. Harding three days after the hotel opened established the resort as an exclusive destination, one that modernist poet Wallace Stevens stayed at frequently from 1922 to 1940. After his first trip to Key West in 1922, Wallace wrote, "It was very much like a cloud full of Cuban senoritas, coconut palms, and waiters carrying ice water. The place is a paradise."

In subsequent decades, the economic vicissitudes of the remote tropical island were like a roller coaster—up in the 1920s during the cigar-making heyday, down in the 30s in the midst of the Great Depression and an insanely intense Category 5 hurricane in 1935, which so completely destroyed Flagler's railroad that it became financially infeasible to restore it, and left Key West the poorest in the nation; up again in the 1940s during the war and in the 50s with the exploding shrimping industry (brought on by Key West's famous "pinks" from the Dry Tortugas shrimp grounds in the Gulf), down in the 60s when Key West was largely a Navy town with few tourists or visitors on Duval Street (the mile-long main street in Key West, running north and south from the Gulf of Mexico to the Atlantic Ocean) and down even more in the 70s when the Key West Naval Station was formally closed in 1974, resulting in a loss of civilian jobs and a severe blow to the economy.

WHEN CAUTHEN ARRIVED in Key West in 1984—the year the Apple Macintosh computer first went on sale; the year many people were just starting to talk about and understand the AIDS crisis—crime in Key West was commonplace, particularly drug trafficking.

But, then, in the early morning hours of June 29, 1984, in

what could have easily been an episode from the 1980s TV crime drama *Miami Vice*, the FBI rounded up a bunch of the bad guys, who happened to include the Deputy Key West Police Chief, two detectives, a veteran of the Key West Fire Department, a former county attorney (who was also co-owner of the Conch Tour Train), and a local school bus driver, among others.

They were arrested (and later convicted by a federal jury) for running a protection racket for drug dealers, as well as for bribery and conspiracy. The cocaine business, according to the indictment, was headquartered at city hall where cocaine was routinely delivered in Burger King bags to the Deputy Police Chief.

For most residents, who were accustomed to public corruption on their tropical paradise, the arrests that morning came as quite a surprise. After all, the island thrived on its live-and-let-live ethos, one that was both tolerant and bohemian, and one that was predicated on a history of welcoming everyone from pirates to poets, renegades to raconteurs, rumrunners to writers.

In what could be considered as a rather humorous aspect of the arrest, according to the indictment the Deputy Police Chief had complained to a co-conspirator that "he was fed up with people doing things in Key West without paying him."

A year later, that same Deputy Police Chief broke into tears in front of the judge in the federal courtroom, as he begged for mercy. He was then sentenced to thirty years in prison.

Despite the arrests, Key West in the early 1980s was like a bad hangover—literally and figuratively—from the wild, wild Key West of the 1970s—a decade that was vividly captured in two of Thomas McGuane's novels, *Ninety-two in the Shade* and *Panama,* where "drug smugglers thrived and cocaine was plentiful, cheap, and more or less, socially acceptable."

"Key West was wide open back then," Billy Cauthen told me, and not any more so than on Duval Street, where a rowdy, Rabelaisian crowd gathered each night and well into the morning hours.

"There was only one or two cops for the whole town of about 25,000 people," Cauthen added. "You could go down to Duval Street and order a beer and line of cocaine, snort a line right on the bar."

Cauthen's first order of business after arriving in Key West was to find a job. So, he headed to Captain Tony's Saloon on Greene Street, located in an old historic building that had started out life in Key West as an ice house and a city morgue. Cauthen knew the manager there and hoped his friend might have some leads on some work.

In 1938 Sloppy Joe's bar moved from its original location on Greene to Duval.

Captain Tony's was the original location of Sloppy Joe's where Ernest Hemingway spent most of his evenings between 1933 (the bar opened its doors on December 5, 1933, the very day Prohibition ended) and 1937. After a dispute about rent that year, the owner of Sloppy Joe's moved the bar to its present location on the corner of Duval and Greene where today tourists fresh off the tourist boat head to find the ghost of Hemingway, when what they actually find is an assortment of t-shirts, sweats, and souvenirs, all adorned with the picture of Papa Hemingway (about as close to his ghost as they'll find). Cauthen plopped himself down on a bar stool at Captain Tony's. Lying on the bar was a copy of the day's *Key West Citizen*, the local newspaper. Below the fold of this August 26 edition was the headline: "Capote Dead at 59." The Capote in the headline was, of course, Truman Capote, a novelist and playwright, author of the novella *Breakfast at Tiffany's*, but who is probably best known for what he labeled a nonfiction novel, *In Cold Blood*.

Capote had first come to Key West in 1968, invited by his friend David Wolkowsky, a man who was more instrumental in launching Key West as a tourist destination than any other.

WOLKOWSKY GREW UP in Key West and Miami, but built his first fortune in Philadelphia as a developer, renovating, restoring and preserving old Philly neighborhoods. Returning to Key West in 1962, Wolkowsky launched his biggest restoration and preservation project of his career and his life, restoring not just a condemned building on Duval Street here or a dilapidated house on Simonton there, but an entire town and in the process, he transformed Key West from "a sleepy, wartime hangover" into a funky, offbeat, unconventional tourist destination.

In 1967, Wolkowsky built the Pier House Motel and Resort (later just the Pier House), located at the Gulf of Mexico and Duval Street, which today is generally recognized as the landmark turning point for Key West. In order to attract tourists, Wolkowsky invited his celebrity friends to the resort, including Truman Capote, who was working on his gossipy novel *Answered Prayers,* a novel that was still not finished nearly twenty years later when Capote died.

Wolkowsky also let some unknown singer with a guitar named Jimmy Buffett sing in the Chart Room Bar at the Pier House, long before Buffett sang about the joys of the laid-back, tropical lifestyle of Key West.

For more than five decades, Wolkowsky continued to preserve and promote the Rock, as locals call it, "not so much the honky-tonk tourist side...but the place where front porches serve as art installations, bike bells replace car horns and night-blooming flowers perfume the air with mystery."

"He's Mr. Key West," said best-selling children's author and longtime Key West resident Judy Blume—an apt sobriquet for a man who made Key West what it is today.

AS SERENDIPITY WOULD HAVE IT, Cauthen met a real estate broker named Charles Lee at Captain Tony's. Lee's business partner, Tom Taylor, was the resident manager of a compound on Windsor Lane in Old Town, where, Lee said, there might be some work.

The compound consisted of eleven homes on an acre of land on Solares Hill, the highest point of land on the island with peak elevation at eighteen feet (5.5 m) above sea level. In his book *The Streets of Key West: A History Through Street Names,* J. Wills Burk (a pseudonym) pinpointed the location of that peak elevation near the former home of Welsh-born theater director and writer Philip Burton on Angela Street, "precisely twelve and a half steps from Whitmarsh Lane." (Burton was the "step-father" and mentor of actor Richard Jenkins, better known as Richard Burton.)

The eight frame houses and three CBS (concrete block stucco) homes in the compound had been built in the 1930s for cigar-makers and their families, but over the years had been abandoned and had fallen into the hands of squatters. "It had become a hippie hangout," one longtime resident told me.

In the early 1970s, a Miami lawyer and real estate developer purchased the property, renovated the homes, many of which at that point were just fallen-down shacks, put in a pool in the center of the compound, and added a 210-foot-long wall to run along the length of the compound on Windsor Lane, guaranteeing the privacy for its occupants behind the double gates. He then offered the homes for sale with a ninety-nine-year lease on the shared land.

It was Charlotte (Charlee, pronounced "Charlie") Wilbur, wife of poet Richard Wilbur, who had originally heard about the compound—no one recalls exactly how—and who encouraged her friends—John Ciardi and his wife Judith, Ralph Ellison and his wife Fanny, and John Hersey and his wife Barbara—to join Dick and her in purchasing a home in the compound.

And by March 1976, each couple owned a little piece of paradise. For nearly three decades, these families spent at least part of the winter living and working in the compound. During this time, their friendships would be tested, even broken, over squabbles both petty and provocative from land disputes to alleged homophobia. But there were also good times with friends both inside and out of the compound, perhaps none so well-known as the weekly anagram games among logophiles of the compound and their friends, immortalized by John Hersey in his short story called "A Game of Anagrams," one of fifteen short stories in *Key West Tales*.

"Go speak to Tom," Charles Lee told Cauthen that afternoon at Captain Tony's. "He may have some work for you in the compound."

Twenty-seven years later, when Cauthen and I sat down to talk about his experiences and recollections of Key West and the famous residents of the compound, he was still working there, doing everything from taking care of general maintenance problems to supervising renovation projects. He had become as much a part of the history of the compound as its famous writers.

THIS GROUP OF FOUR WRITERS who owned homes in the compound weren't the first writers to discover the charm and mystique of Key West, of course. Decades earlier, John Dos Passos, a member of the Lost Generation of writers, who is best known for his *U.S.A. Trilogy* (ranked 23rd on Modern Library's 1998 list of the 100 Best English-language novels of the 20th century) got the literary writers-in-residence ball rolling.

In the late 1920s, Passos, who owned a home at 1401 Pine Street in what today is known as the Meadows near Eisenhower Drive

Ernest Hemingway (left) and John Dos Passos pose with two tarpon fish, Key West, FL, 1928.

and Truman Avenue, suggested to his friend Ernest Hemingway that he give Key West a try if he was looking for a warm place to "dry out his bones." As a result, Hemingway made his first visit to the island in March 1928 and according to Dave Gonzales, director at the Ernest Hemingway House and Museum, "he fell in love with Key West."

And so Hemingway kept coming back with his second wife, Pauline. In 1931, Pauline's uncle bought a Spanish colonial home at 907 Whitehead Street near the southern coast of the island, and he gave it to the couple as a belated wedding gift. (They had been married four years by then.)

The home was originally built in 1851 by the owner of a large salvaging operation, but in later years had been abandoned, making it possible for Pauline's uncle to purchase the home from the city for $8,000 in back taxes (about $122,000 in 2018). Hemingway and his wife Pauline and their two small children lived in the home from 1931 to 1939, during which time he wrote *To Have and Have Not* as well as the short story *The Snows of Kilimanjaro*. Today, the property is almost more famous for its dozens of polydactyl (six-toed) cats, some reportedly descendants of Snow White, a six-toed cat given to Hemingway by a sea captain.

Soon, other writers followed. modernist poet Wallace Stevens wintered at the Casa Marina resort throughout the 1920s and 30s. Robert Frost rented a small cottage behind a building at 410 Caroline Street from 1941 to 1960. Poet and short-story writer Elizabeth Bishop bought a clapboard eyebrow home (a style unique to Key West named for upper windows shaded by the roof overhang) at 624 White Street in 1938 at the age of twenty-seven, where she lived for the next nine years with her then partner Louise Crane and later Marjorie Stevens, neither relationship of which lasted very long probably, in part, because of Bishop's alcoholism.

During her stay in Key West, Bishop published her first volume of poems, *North and South,* in 1946.

Over the course of the next half century, dozens of other writers bought homes in Key West, including James Leo Herlihy, author of *Midnight Cowboy,* in the 60s; playwright Tennessee Williams who visited and lived in Key West from 1941 until his death in 1983 (buying a Bahamian cottage at 1431 Duncan in 1950); and Terrence McNally, winner of the Tony Award for Best Play for *Love! Valour! Compassion!* and *Master Class,* as well as Best Book of a Musical for *Kiss of the Spider Woman* and *Ragtime,* who had a home in Key West in the 90s.

Of course, there were other lesser-known but still accomplished writers who found inspiration in Key West, including Christopher Cox, who in 1983, at age thirty-three, wrote *A Key West Companion.* Both novelist Alison Lurie and poet Richard Wilbur praised the book. Wilbur called it "infinitely superior to the usual guidebook. It shuffles together, in its brisk and evocative essays, phases of the island's curious history, glimpses of its architecture, traditions, and human variety, anecdotes of the eminent, interviews with the obscure, and the lore of everything from sponge-harvesting to voodoo. It leaves one with a keen atmospheric sense of the place."

WHAT DREW THESE WRITERS and so many other authors, artists, publishers, agents, and composers to Key West? "Terrence McNally will say there is something in the air," said Judith Daykin, a longtime compound resident, when we talked about the allure of Key West in her totally cozy and charming cigar-maker's cottage in the compound. "He once told me he just felt different when he was down here. 'I can write better, more easily and freely,' he said." It was a feeling shared by many other writers living in Key West.

Alison Lurie had a similar response when I asked her the same question one January morning at the home she shares with her novelist husband, author Edward Hower, on Reynolds. "Key West was always a very tolerant society," said the soft-spoken Lurie.

"Nobody looked at you disapprovingly because of what you wore or what you said or how you lived or who you loved. There was a kind of freedom."

Lurie had purchased her first home in Key West in 1979, nearly twenty years after the publication of her first novel *Love and Friendship* at the age of thirty-six. The story, often described as social satire, was not unlike her own story as a student at Radcliffe College in Cambridge, MA, during the war. It chronicled the lives of a group of young people living in a small college town. "The book was well received," said Lurie, "considering I was an unknown."

That first home, Lurie said, was a "tiny little house on Stump Lane off White Street. Charlee [Wilbur] wanted us to buy in the compound, but there wasn't anything available," she continued. "There wasn't much turnover in the compound; people who settled there liked it."

As we talked on that pleasant January morning, Lurie reminisced about "the good old days." Money didn't matter very much, either, Lurie continued. "There was no feeling you had to have more money or you had to spend more money, you had to dress properly. It was a very freeing sense."

Lynn Kaufelt, author with Jeffrey Cardenas of *Key West Writers and Their Houses*, would agree. "At a party here," she once said, "the mayor might come in a polyester suit, and the sheriff, and some Cubans, and some gays, and John

Ciardi, and Richard Wilbur. It's a wonderful thing."

Lynn first came to Key West in 1975 with her husband, author David Kaufelt, right after his debut novel *Six Months with an Older Woman* was published. For the first few years, the couple lived in Key West for six months of the year and then six months in Sag Harbor, Long Island, NY. Sag Harbor, a former whaling village in the early 1800s, was a community with its own history of writers, including James Fenimore Cooper and Walt Whitman in the 1800s, and later, after the war, with Kurt Vonnegut, E.L. Doctorow, John Knowles, and John Steinbeck, who was noted for his love of Sag Harbor, and had a home there from 1955 until his death in 1968. Forty years later, David Margolick, author of numerous nonfiction books including *Elizabeth and Hazel: Two Women of Little Rock,* bought a small home on the bay in Sag Harbor.

In Key West, the Kaufelts had a home in a compound called Conch Grove, a six-unit compound on Catherine and Varela. It was the same compound where James Kirkwood, author of *P.S. Your Cat Is Dead* and *There Must Be a Pony*, had a home, as did longtime Dell/Delacorte publisher Ross Claiborne, who had published Kaufelt's first book. In addition, New York literary agent J.S. (Jay) Garon, the man who "discovered" author John Grisham after Grisham's first novel had been turned down by more than thirty agents, kept a winter home in the Conch Grove compound.

"I love the fact that Key West has this terrific author presence," said Claiborne, who was responsible for bringing a lot of writers down in the early days before it was discovered. He was also actively involved in the first Key West Literary Seminar, founded by David and Lynn Kaufelt in 1983.

The four-day writers' conference explores a unique literary theme each January and draws some of the best writers both known and unknown from around the world. According to David Kaufelt, the idea for the seminar came about when literary agent Dick Duane and Kaufelt were "schmoozing over Diet Cokes and white meat chicken sandwiches" in a Manhattan hotel bar with Rosemary Jones of the Council for Florida Libraries. "Jones was in New York to round up authors for the council's annual lecture series," Kaufelt said. "But New York publishers' publicists were having none of it, fully convinced no one in Florida read, much less bought books."

So, Kaufelt suggested that since there were so many writers of so many persuasions in Key West, they could have their own literary festival. "There was a sudden enlightened silence," Kaufelt said. "We could. We should. And we would." And they did.

The first Key West Literary Seminar was held in January 1983. Literary agents Dick Duane and Robert (Bob) Thixton hosted a cocktail party at their stunning Key West residence during the seminar. John Ciardi gave a presentation on "Poetry and Language" at a dinner at the Casa Marina. And David Kaufelt conducted the first Key West Literary Tour, a walking tour of the homes of famous Key West writers—an event that to this day continues to be a popular activity during the Seminar.

IN ADDITION TO A LAISSEZ-FAIRE ATTITUDE, Key West exuded a quieter vibe back in the 1970s and early 80s. It was before the cruise ships started to dump tens of thousands of tourists onto Duval each year (more than 750,000 in 2017, as well as an additional 375,000 who arrived by air), all eager to take part in the funky, exotic, unconventional Key West experience (and buy a few t-shirts and trinkets along the way); it was before Calvin Klein bought the first million-dollar house at 712 Eaton, one of only two octagon houses in Key West; it was before Key West hosted the first annual Fantasy Fest, the absolutely insane ten-day "party for grown-ups."

Those things would come, of course, much to the chagrin of Lurie and others who reveled in their tropical hideaway. Yet, it wasn't the first time a writer would find the changes in Key West disheartening. As early as 1940, Wallace Stevens wrote to a friend about how Key West was changing. "Key West is no longer quite the delightful affectation it once was," Stevens wrote from the Casa Marina hotel. "Who wants to share green cocoanut ice cream with these strange monsters who snooze in the porches of this once forlorn hotel?"

"We made a mistake," said Lurie, referring to herself and other writers at that time. "We all started writing articles about how wonderful Key West was. That attracted the rich people. They bought big houses and started giving big parties. We had come to work; the rich people came to enjoy themselves."

In 1986, James Kirkwood explained to a reporter that back in the 60s, "if someone had dropped you down in Key West and you didn't know where you were and looked around, you would probably think you were on some Caribbean island. But now you get more of a Coconut Groveish, a West Palm Beach—that flavor."

That change came about, according to poet Richard Wilbur, because the developers of Key West—the people who wanted to popularize it— "began to glamorize it as a haven for writers, as a place where Hemingway had worked and where all sorts of lesser writers were still to be seen in the flesh."

Today, despite the many changes over the years, Key West

is still a haven for writers. What is it that attracts so many to this tropical island?

Author David Kaufelt had one theory. He called his idea the Peter Pan theory. "Freud said that we are at our most creative when we are in our very early youth," Kaufelt explained, "before we're five years old. That's where we are here. We wear shorts, we ride bicycles, we have the water, a great symbol of the unconscious, and we're free to be children here and let our spirits go."

Free to let our spirits go: No doubt it's what has attracted so many writers to this six-square-mile island for nearly a century now. They came, and many stayed, having discovered what Jimmy Buffett wrote about the island in his now classic 1973 song about Key West where "none of the streets look the same."

"You can have the rest of everything I own
'Cause I have found me a home."

CHAPTER 1

JOHN CIARDI

A Man's Man

Photograph by LaVerne Harrell Clark, courtesy of The University of Arizona Poetry Center.
Photograph copyright © 1973 Arizona Board of Regents.

"The essential kindness of the man was not
displayed casually, as a social grace; thus, it
sometimes went unperceived."

-- Vince Clemente,
John Ciardi: Measure of the Man

Chapter 1

JOHN CIARDI

IT WAS COLD IN METUCHEN, NJ, about twenty-one degrees Fahrenheit, typical for a January day in this small community of about 12,000 people, twenty-one miles southwest of Manhattan, but way too cold for sixty-year-old John Ciardi (char-dee). The cold weather made him antsy and agitated. He was ready to get out of the North and head south to his winter home in Key West, where his tired bones could dry out and he could enjoy "sun-drenched breakfasts on the patio."

"I'm ready to sit in Florida, take off my clothes, spit out these choppers, gum my mush, and just lie in the sun," he told his wife, Judith.

So, on January 15, 1977, Ciardi and Judith packed up their Oldsmobile 98 sedan, jumped on I-95 a few miles from Metuchen, and headed south for the three-day, fifteen-hundred-mile trip to the southernmost point of the continental United States. Their trip would take them through six states before he reached Florida, many which offered great opportunities for historic sightseeing, including the Jamestown Settlement Museum in Williamsburg and the Civil War mansions in Savannah, GA, but such sightseeing excursions would have to wait until another time, if ever.

By late afternoon that first day, they had made it to Rocky Mount, North Carolina, a distance of about 450 miles from Metuchen, and a town best known, perhaps, as the birth place in 1917 of jazz pianist and composer Thelonious Monk.

The second day, a slightly longer drive got them to Jacksonville, Florida, where the weather was finally starting to warm up, and Ciardi's chilled bones started to thaw.

The third day of their journey took them past many beautiful coastal towns including St. Augustine, Daytona Beach, and West Palm Beach. As they passed Fort Lauderdale, Ciardi opened the window to take in the warm sweet smells of a quick rain shower they had passed through. The sweet, fresh, pungent smell of ozone filled the air as the winds picked up and clouds rolled in, heralding another approaching thundershower.

Finally, around 4:00 in the afternoon on the third day, they crossed over the Cow Channel from Stock Island to Key West, turned south on Route 1, and headed into the home stretch, as the warm trade winds told them they were almost home.

They drove down Roosevelt Boulevard across White Street, where Roosevelt becomes Truman Avenue, to Elizabeth Street where the historic Conch House had stood since 1889, first as a private home and today a bed-and-breakfast. There, he turned right onto the very narrow street that would take him past 815 Elizabeth and the Church of God of Prophesy, and past 702 Elizabeth, the home of his neighbor, poet James Merrill and his partner David Jackson.

From out of nowhere as they traveled the short distance across Elizabeth, a red moped with two teenage boys sped around them on the narrow street causing Ciardi to curse under his breath but loud enough for Judith to hear. "Crazy kids," he said. "They shouldn't be allowed on those things." Judith didn't respond, but sat quietly by his side, her pursed lips the only giveaway to what she may have been thinking.

At the corner of Elizabeth, Ciardi turned right onto

Windsor Lane, a tiny street at the top of Solares Hill that cuts diagonally from Elizabeth to the historic 1847 Key West Cemetery located, some say, "dead" center in Old Town, the cemetery where one epitaph proclaims, "I told you I was sick."

Midway down Windsor Lane, the Olds 98 came to the double wooden gates to the compound's entrance. They were home—home where giant palms and avocado trees touched the beautiful blue sky, and the smell of night-blooming jasmine filled the evening air. And where breakfast on a sun-drenched patio was waiting.

"I am in a green paradise," Ciardi wrote to a friend that season. "The sun is bright, the day tropical, and a sea breeze blows in from Cuba, which is only 90 miles away. I think this piece of the world is beautiful. I like what I feel and see, and I have a friend to tell about it. I think I am happy."

JUDITH MYRA HOSTETTER had been by Ciardi's side now for thirty years, ever since, as a journalism instructor at the University of Kansas (now the University of Missouri-Kansas City), she was asked to interview a "returning hero" from the war who had just accepted a teaching position at the university. She had been warned, though, to be careful, since the "hero" was a "brash young man."

As Ciardi recalled years later, she "dutifully watched out for me all through the interview, and that night at dinner, and the next night, and the next, and through the semester." And in July 1946 they were married.

Now, as they pulled up to the compound on Windsor Lane that January afternoon, she was still "watching out for him." As one compound resident said, "You couldn't help but feel Judith was the stabilizing force behind this bigger-than-life poet."

In many ways, Judith was like the three extraordinary women British writer Edna Healey wrote about in *Wives of Fame* —all wives of more famous men: David Livingstone, one of the most popular British heroes of the late nineteenth century, Karl Marx, the German philosopher and revolutionary socialist, and Charles Darwin, the English biologist best known for his theory of evolution.

In her book, Healey wrote, "Often there stands a wife, invisible and forgotten, whose name is not recorded on the tablets of bronze and of whose famous husband it is so frequently said, 'I didn't know he had a wife.'" That was Judith Myra Hostetter Ciardi.

"Because Ciardi was so big and noisy and boisterous," said author Alison Lurie, "there wasn't much space for Judith. He took up so much room, but Judith accepted him, even enjoyed him."

Of course, part of the success of her marriage to a man who was bigger than life must have had to do with Judith's own sense of humor. Once, a graduate student whom both Judith and John had gotten to know and who was visiting in their home commented that her coffee tasted like jet fuel to which she quickly responded that it was necessary in order to jump-start John's heart every morning.

JOHN AND JUDITH HAD BOUGHT their Key West house—a shack, really, according to Ciardi—the previous year in February 1976 for $19,000. Built in the 1930s, the home originally was a two-room cigar-maker's cottage. Over time, the cottage had been enlarged to four rooms, still tiny compared to the Ciardis' fourteen-room home on two acres in Metuchen, a town known by the locals as the "brainy boro," since it was home to dozens of artists, educators, and literary figures who had settled there over the years.

Unlike Hersey and Ellison's houses in the compound, both of which faced Windsor Lane behind a white stucco wall, Ciardi's house sat way back in the compound property, behind and to the north of the pool, and completely hidden from view from the main gate.

Over the course of the next nine years, Ciardi would sell the original cigar-maker's cottage, buy another home in the compound only a few yards away, sell it, and finally build a home on a piece of land that was *in* the compound but not *part* of the compound—a situation that would eventually lead to the most contentious scuffle that confronted the famous homeowners.

"HOW DID YOU BECOME A POET?" It was a question John Ciardi was asked a lot, whether in academic seminars around the country, at cocktail parties in Metuchen or Key West, or, as in this case, at the local Key West High School on Flagler Street where he was a frequent and popular guest speaker. The question came up in a Question and Answer session during the school's Local Authors series.

"I don't know how I actually started writing," Ciardi said in a gravelly voice that no doubt resulted in part from his three-pack-a-day cigarette habit. "At what point does a social drinker become an alcoholic?" he asked his young audience rhetorically. "Writing is not as much something you do, it is the way you live."

And, for sure, writing poetry was the way Ciardi had lived now for nearly fifty years. As a teenager in the rural town of Medford, MA, six miles northwest of Boston (on a street that runs parallel to the Mystic River, the river referred to in the 1844 poem "Over the River and Through the Woods"), Ciardi inexplicably began prowling the stacks of Medford's public library, discovering a range of poets. He read *Spoon*

River Anthology, a collection of short free-form poems by Edgar Lee Masters; he read the poems and stories by Rudyard Kipling; he read *The Man with the Hoe* by Edwin Markham.

Ciardi also read the works of a young American lyrical poet named Edna St. Vincent Millay, a poet with whom, at the time, he was totally entranced, quoting her poems often by heart ("What lips my lips have kissed and where, and why/I have forgotten. . . .") but whom he would later vilify in a review of her life and work, saying it "appealed only to the adolescent mind."

But it was at Tufts College (now Tufts University) in Medford that an event changed the rest of his life. He signed up for a course by a young professor who, according to Ciardi, understood poetry in ways that few others did. "What he knew about was the *insides* of a poem," Ciardi later explained. "What he lived was the happy excitement of each living poem as he found it. And he knew how to transmit that excitement and make it real."

Ciardi signed up for his writing course and knew almost at once what he wanted to do with the rest of his life. "I had no idea what I would do for food and shelter," he said, "...but what I would live for was poetry." And so he did.

During his life as a poet, John Ciardi wrote more than fifteen books of poetry, produced three etymological dictionaries, and wrote three volumes of limericks with his friend Isaac Asimov. (The first book—*Limericks: Too Gross*—became such an instant success that the publisher immediately asked for a second edition.) Ciardi was a master of limericks, said friend and author Elly Welt. "He would invent a limerick at the slightest provocation."

Ciardi and Asimov, one of the major science fiction writers of the twentieth century, known for his *Foundation* series, were best friends, perhaps in part because they both enjoyed a linguistic competitiveness. "They would take turns insulting each other in dead languages," said Ciardi's youngest son Benn. Asimov was a longtime member of Mensa International. "What my father didn't know, Asimov knew."

During his life, Ciardi also wrote dozens of essays (his bon mots and epigrammatic comments were legendary). Perhaps his greatest literary achievement, though, was his translation of Dante's *Divine Comedy*—a massive undertaking that took him sixteen years to complete, and which today is considered by many to be the most readable translation of this fourteenth century narrative poem since Henry Wadsworth Longfellow's translation in 1867.

Ciardi was by his own admission a workaholic. "I love the work obsessively and am at the same time afraid it is consuming me. Sanity says I should ration my hours more wisely, but obsession wins."

"What does it take to be a good writer?"

It was the last question in the Q&A session at the high school's Local Authors series. "Being fascinated by words is essential," he told the crowd. He then added in his own humorous way, "In addition, as Robert Frost said, 'You must have a bright idea.'" If the comment seemed flippant, as it possibly did, given his often-gruff demeanor, no one seemed to notice.

YET FOR ALL HIS ACCOMPLISHMENTS as a poet, John Ciardi was still considered by many of his contemporaries as just an average writer. "All of the other three writers who lived in the compound," said novelist Alison Lurie, "were extremely good writers, but Ciardi was just an okay writer. He was a good speaker, though. He told a lot of jokes, got the audience laughing. Unlike Ralph [Ellison] who hated being a public figure and didn't make any effort to draw attention to himself, Ciardi loved being in the public eye and relished being the center of attention."

By the early 1980s, it was "fashionable to consider John Ciardi a poet long past his prime," an opinion that Ciardi was well aware of. Yet, he hoped that a new volume of verse called *Selected Poems*, published in 1984, would restore his reputation as an important contemporary American poet.

It didn't.

In June 1985 a young poet and critic named David Wojahn wrote a review in *Poetry* magazine about *Selected Poems*. Wojahn had developed a reputation over the years of being rather brutal in his criticisms and his review of *Selected Poems* lived up to his reputation. It was harsh, even nasty, not only about the poetry but about Ciardi himself. Wojahn called Ciardi "smug and self-important" and asserted that Ciardi was "mostly just a crank."

Wojahn concluded his assessment by noting that Ciardi's section of love poems "come close to being greeting card verse." Of course, he wasn't far from wrong. One love poem expressed this Hallmark-like sentiment that would have caused even Edna St. Vincent Millay to blanch.

Some of the best everywhere are waiting always/

for less than happens every time you smile.

In face of the scathing and deeply personal review by Wojahn, Ciardi once again put on a stoic exterior. "I have stopped complaining about the world I never made," he said.

Twenty-six years later, perhaps with a perspective that only comes with age and maturity, Wojahn confessed that perhaps he was too harsh in his criticism of Ciardi, a man he never met. "The piece was decidedly arch and snide," Wojahn said, "but I can't say it was wholly inaccurate in its appraisal of Ciardi's work."

CIARDI, OVERWEIGHT AND TIRED-LOOKING wearing a loose-fitting green Hawaiian shirt and khaki shorts, was sitting by the pool in the center of the compound with his friends and compound neighbors, Dick Wilbur and John Hersey. He popped open a bottle of champagne to celebrate the fact that he had just finished writing Volume 1 of *A Browser's Dictionary: A Compendium of Curious Expressions & Intriguing Facts* about the origins and histories of words and phrases in the English language, a book that would firmly establish him as a most irreverent lexicographer.

For Ciardi, a bottle of bourbon—his liquor of choice and, by all accounts, one he chose way too often—might have been more appropriate for the celebration. He often still griped about a White House reception during Jimmy Carter's administration where the only liquor that was served was Chardonnay, unlike a Lyndon Johnson reception fifteen years earlier where there was plenty of bourbon to go around.

Ciardi had known Wilbur and Hersey since his days at Bread Loaf, a writer's conference in Middlebury, Vermont. It was there in 1959 that he also met future compound resident Ralph Ellison, author of *Invisible Man.*

Bread Loaf was founded in 1926 as a way for older, more established writers to help new writers on their way to fame. Ciardi had been invited to attend the Bread Loaf conference for the first time in August 1940 at the age of twenty-four, along with another young writer, the fragile, androgynous Carson McCullers, whose first novel *The Heart Is a Lonely Hunter* would soon bring her worldwide fame, as well as Eudora Welty, who would win a Pulitzer Prize in 1973 for her novel *The Optimist's Daughter.*

Seven years later, Ciardi was invited to join the faculty at Bread Loaf, and eventually, in 1956 he was named Executive Director of the Bread Loaf conference, a position he held for fifteen years until he was unceremoniously booted out after ongoing battles with the assistant director over certain policies regarding the running of the conference.

He learned he had been fired as Executive Director through a press release that was sent out to the local newspapers just before the beginning of the August 1972 conference, a situation not unlike being fired by Twitter in 2018.

The dismissal left him hurt, angry, and bitter. "I am left with a sense of having played a stupidly amateur role among professional politicians," he said in a letter to the president of Middlebury College, which administered the Bread Loaf conference.

Typically, at the departure of the Executive Director, there would have been a special dinner or appreciation ceremony, but Ciardi would have none of it. "I ask that there be no ceremonial gestures in honor of my services to Bread Loaf," he wrote to Armstrong. "Your more practical estimate has been rendered. I must accept it, and I would have to reject any other as window dressing."

Having poured a glass of champagne for his fellow writers at the pool, Ciardi lit up a Vantage cigarette, one of dozens he would have that day. He once confessed to smoking three packs a day "mostly because there isn't time in a day to smoke more than that (and what the hell, it's too late for me to die young)."

For years his cigarette of choice had been Lark, but he had recently switched to Vantage because he wanted a lower-tar cigarette. He had thought about quitting—thought about it dozens of times—even gave it up entirely a few times, only to pick up a cigarette a few days later. So, the least he could do, he thought, was to lower the nicotine and tar in the cigarettes he smoked.

As usual, Ciardi's conversation that afternoon at the pool was all about Ciardi. Even outside, in the open air, he somehow managed to suck up all the oxygen as he expounded on a variety of topics—his senior citizen status ("I used to smoke and drink between acts of sex; now I have more time for smoking and drinking"); the raising of his children ("I think son Jonnel is planning to sue us for malpractice with himself as the conclusive evidence"); the irony of his book sales ("I got a royalty statement this week. *Divine Comedy* sold a grand total of 258 books; *Limericks: Too Gross* sold 12,548 copies!"); even drinking, ("There is nothing wrong with sobriety in moderation").

As one compound resident put it derisively, "Ciardi had the ability to strut while sitting." Author Edward Hower, husband of Alison Lurie, had a different take on the man, however. "Ciardi was a show-off," he said, "but not necessarily in a bad way. He was always talking, telling jokes; he was a raconteur. He liked to drop names. It was fun to listen to him."

FOR THE MOST PART, the compound ran smoothly during those early years, which, according to longtime resident Tom Wilson, was a bit odd given the personalities. "Everyone pretty much got along," Wilson said, "even if there was an occasional disagreement or a snippy comment (behind someone's back) about one thing or another. The only thing I remember being an issue one year was about getting a new lock on the gate."

There was, however, one major issue centered around Ciardi that went on for years. It had to do with a parcel of land that was physically *in* the compound but was never made *part* of the compound.

Apparently, when the developer of the compound created

the Windsor Village Condominium Association, he maintained ownership of the land but leased it to the condominium association. "You bought your house, fee simple, subject to a ninety-nine-year lease," explained Charles Lee, manager of the compound starting in the early 90s.

But the developer also kept one parcel of land for himself at the back of the compound that was not part of the condominium association, as well as a five-foot-wide egress/ingress from the front gate to his land in the rear, where he planned to build a house. "His plan was to live in the compound without having to pay association dues," Lee said.

But then the developer changed his mind about what he wanted to do with the parcel and sold the land and the easement to Ciardi. In turn, Ciardi built a house on the property which he began using in 1980. That set the stage for what would become an ongoing dispute between Ciardi and the other homeowners and, later, between Ciardi's daughter, Myra, and the homeowners' association.

"Ciardi felt that because his house was within the confines of the compound, he should be able to enjoy the amenities of the compound, such as the swimming pool," Lee explained. "But at the same time, since his property was not technically *part* of the compound, he didn't think he should have to pay association dues."

Needless to say, the other compound home owners disagreed. They pointed out that he was benefitting from such things as the swimming pool, as well as maintenance of the grounds, gardening services, and even trash collection without paying an association fee.

Ciardi also felt he should be able to drive his car on that five-foot- wide strip of land from the front of the compound to his house. "When John Hersey heard what Ciardi planned to do as far as driving his car into the compound," said Lee, "he threw a hissy fit. He rushed out to measure the width of Ciardi's Oldsmobile and proclaimed to Ciardi that there was not enough room on the five-foot easement for him to drive his car down the path."

But that didn't stop Ciardi. "He went out, jumped in the car, raced the engine, and zoomed down the path, ripping out plants along the way," said Lee.

So, that was the beginning of the bickering over the land and association dues that went for years without any real resolution. "Ciardi was by far the most irascible about the situation," said Wilson. "Every year, he would launch into this thing about putting a fence down the middle of the property."

To some residents, it all seemed like just a big game between Hersey and Ciardi than anything else. "Each was flexing his muscle," said Dick Reynolds, a longtime compound resident. "The rest of us in the compound would hear them bickering and just think, 'Oh, they're at it again.' Personally, I think they were just putting on a little act for the rest of us."

Other residents of the compound, however, remember the turf war differently. "There was a lot of rancor between Hersey and Ciardi over the easement," Daykin said. "In the end, they didn't speak much."

Even though the issue was never completely resolved, and even though it continued to raise its ugly head once or twice a year with Ciardi's daughter, Myra, over time the animosity just kind of quietly dissipated. "Eventually, everybody kind of let the issue die," Lee said, "and life went on."

The only other issue that came up during those years, apparently, was in the early 90s when the developer, who still owned all of the common element, decided he wanted to sell the land and contacted the home owners to see if they wanted to buy. They did.

So, for about $12,000 each, as Lee recalled, the home owners got together and bought all of the common element—all of the compound property that an owner's home wasn't already sitting on.

But that set off what became known among the compound home owners as "The Big Land Grab." Everyone tried to stake out more land around their home than what was legally theirs. As a result, almost everybody got more footage as part of their property.

It was all done very surreptitiously, Wilson said. One owner got common land under a deck she had built. Another owner appropriated land from a footpath that ran past his house.

"Dick and Charlee put up a stockade fence around some of the common property adjacent to their house," Wilson said, "thereby expanding the size of their own property." Even Wilson appropriated a tiny patio on the side of his house that was originally part of the common element by simply putting a fence around it and claiming the property as part of his home.

DURING THE WINTER SEASON, there were always social activities that kept Ciardi busy—plays, lectures, cocktail parties, dinners, and concerts. One evening during the 1979/80 season, he and Judith attended a concert by a man Ciardi called one of the giants of the piano—a classical pianist from Russia, Lasar Berman.

Berman was famous, in part, for refusing to play Chopin. "Of course, I used to play him," he once remarked, "but many years ago I entered a Chopin competition and I did not qualify. It was an awful blow to my pride, and I vowed that I would never play him again." True to his word, he never did.

There were, of course, numerous theater productions to see each season, whether at the Red Barn Theater on Duval, the Waterfront Theater on Mallory Square, or beginning in 1980, the Tennessee Williams Fine Arts Center, situated on the campus of Florida Keys Community College, which opened its doors for the first time in conjunction with the world premiere of Williams' little-known play, "Will Mr. Merriweather Return from Memphis?" —a play Williams had originally written in 1969.

The Red Barn Theater had started life in 1829 as a carriage house, but in the 1940s, a group of actors turned the carriage house into a small theater. Later, the group of actors moved to the Waterfront Playhouse on Mallory Square, where today comedies, dramas, and musical productions are staged each season, featuring internationally known performers, and where tourists and conchs alike gather each evening to watch the sun go down, a nightly event that turns a sunset into performance art.

Ciardi also loved visiting his "winter season" friends. One friend was Philip Burton, who owned a small house on Angela Street, a short walk from the compound. Ciardi would go frequently to share a glass of sherry and talk about everything from poetry to politics.

As Burton recalled, "John always had to have an audience. Even when he grumbled—and he grumbled a lot—he did so with such wit that my response was not a sign of sympathy, but a chuckle."

Two other friends Ciardi visited frequently were James (Jimmy) Merrill and David Jackson. Merrill—the son of the cofounder of the Merrill Lynch brokerage firm—was one of the leading poets of his generation and the recipient of numerous literary awards, including the Bollingen Prize in

1973 and a Pulitzer Prize for Poetry for his *Divine Comedies* in 1977, something that must have secretly gnawed at Ciardi, since he had never received a Pulitzer, as had so many of his friends and colleagues including his compound neighbor Richard Wilbur. (Wilbur was awarded the Pulitzer Prize twice in his career—the first time in 1957 for *Things of This World* and again in 1989 for *New and Collected Poems*, which included virtually all of Wilbur's poetry at that time.)

Poet James Merrill (left) and his partner David Jackson.

Nevertheless, Ciardi claimed it was no big deal. "I never much respected it," he once told a friend. "Nor have I ever much rated with prize judges."

Children's poet Shel Silverstein, who lived in a renovated Greek revival house around the corner from the compound on William Street, was another friend Ciardi visited frequently. "He is a beautiful gent and a brilliant one," Ciardi said.

Beginning in the 1980s, friends and associates, including longtime friend Elly Welt, author of *Berlin Wild*, started to notice and comment on how irascible Ciardi was becoming—more so, than usual, that is. He had always tended to be a grouch, sometimes even a cruel grouch, as evidenced in his 1957 review of a new book of poetry by Anne Morrow Lindbergh, wife of aviator Charles Lindbergh.

"Mrs. Lindbergh has written an offensively bad book," Ciardi wrote in the January 12, 1957 issue of *Saturday Review*, adding that he found her collection of poems on love, loss, and beauty filled with "inexcusable clichés, inappropriate or unexplained metaphors, forced rhymes, and, to top it off, bad grammar." In his frustration, Ciardi scolded Lindbergh with the admonition that "freshman English students are required to take remedial courses when they persist in such illiteracies."

One night in 1985 Judith and John decided to go out to dinner with the Wilburs and others at a popular restaurant called Claire's on Duval Street in Key West. A sculptor named Ilse Getz was at the restaurant. She was, by all accounts, an egomaniac who spoke constantly of herself and had alienated herself from the inner circle of the Key West literary society.

Ciardi simply couldn't tolerate the woman, largely because of her enormous ego, matched only, some would say, by Ciardi's own ego. Yet, somehow, that night she was seated for dinner next to Ciardi, an egregious mistake in good judgment. Within minutes, the two were arguing. No one could recall exactly what the argument was about, but the shouting and name-calling eventually became too much for Ilse, who ran out of the restaurant and, some say, off the island entirely.

When told about this incident, Judith Daykin, who wasn't at the dinner that night, acknowledged that she would never want to be in Ciardi's line of fire, like Ilse. "I'm sure he eviscerated her," she said. "He was sort of the Norman Mailer of his generation. He was extremely difficult to be with. He was very self-focused and into himself and puffed up."

But then, Daykin added, as so many other friends and

acquaintances of Ciardi's always did, "Yet, we always found him fun to be around—extremely entertaining and funny and gregarious."

Ciardi's wife, however, was mortified by her husband's behavior that evening and according to reports, when they got home they had the biggest quarrel of their married life during which she told him in no uncertain terms exactly how disgraceful his outburst had been.

[Post Mortem: Seven years later, Ilse and her husband were found dead of acute carbon monoxide toxicity in what police termed a murder/suicide. Ms. Getz had been suffering from advanced Alzheimer's disease.]

During the past couple of years, Ciardi's health had deteriorated to the point he had trouble getting through airport terminals without a wheelchair. Doctors called it diabetic neuropathy. "I call it a pain in the ass," he said. He could hardly make the walk from his house in the compound to the mailboxes by the front gate, a distance of less than one hundred yards, without having to sit down.

At sixty-nine, Ciardi found himself consulting the actuarial tables frequently, and dwelling on just how much time he might have left on this earth. "The actuarial tables give me plus or minus ten more years, perhaps a little longer if I stop smoking," he said, "but having been a chain smoker for almost fifty-five years now, I am satisfied to die of my own bad habits and pray only to escape my death as a result of someone else's."

THE 1985/86 WINTER SEASON in Key West had evaporated far too quickly, and now as the middle of March approached, John and Judith figured it was time to head back up north. As lovely as the winter season was in this tropical paradise, summer's unrelenting heat and stifling humidity were far more than either one could tolerate. (The average dew point in summer reaches 75 percent or higher, making Key West the most humid city in Florida and Florida the most humid state in the U.S.)

So, on a pleasant March day, they prepared to depart for Metuchen, leaving just weeks before the amazing frangipani tree—the proverbial "ugly duckling" in winter—erupted with its bright summer blooms into a panoply of color. An early morning thunderstorm had passed over the island that morning, not unlike the bewitching thunderstorm in Elizabeth Bishop's haunting but calming poem "Little Exercise at 4:00 A.M," leaving the island "uninjured, barely disturbed."

And so it was in Key West that early morning in March. Judith, who would be forced to drive the whole way back to Metuchen, since her husband was not feeling well, took one last look in the rearview mirror as they pulled away from the compound, not knowing, of course, it would be the last time her husband would see his tropical paradise.

Two weeks later, on March 30, 1986, Easter Sunday, Ciardi was in his den in Metuchen, while Judith busied herself in the kitchen. She thought he was dozing in front of the TV, but when she went to check on him, he was dead.

At a memorial service later that year, Judith spoke about the many titles her husband carried throughout his life— professor, critic, translator, lexicographer, essayist, lecturer, teacher, writer of children's books. But, in the end, Judith said at the memorial service, when all the accolades have subsided, he would have been most pleased to be introduced simply as John Ciardi, poet.

Ciardi on Writing

"Let the action speak for itself. One of the skills of a good poet is to enact his experiences rather than to talk about having had them. *'Show it, don't tell it; make it happen, don't talk about its happening.'*"

~ **John Ciardi,** *How Does a Poem Mean?*

A Day at the Beach
John Ciardi (sitting, fourth from left) joined other Key West writers for this photo on Hidden Beach, Key West, in 1984.

From top left: James Merrill, Evan Rhodes, Edward Hower, Alison Lurie, Shel Silverstein, Bill Manville, Joseph Lash, Arnold Sundgaard, John Williams, Richard Wilbur, Jim Boatwright. **From bottom left:** Susan Nadler, Thomas McGuane, William Wright, John Ciardi, David Kaufelt, Philip Caputo, Philip Burton, John Malcolm Brinnin. *Photo courtesy of Alison Lurie; Photographer: Don Kincaid*

RALPH ELLISON
Renaissance Man

t

"He saw the predicament of blacks in America as a metaphor for the universal human challenge of finding a viable identity in a chaotic and sometimes indifferent world."

-- Anne Seidlitz, American Masters, NPR

Chapter 2

RALPH ELLISON

IT WAS MARCH 1985. Seventy-two-year-old Ralph Ellison emerged from the back door of his winter home on Windsor Lane in Key West early in the morning. Slightly overweight, unlike the slim, fit physique of his youth, Ellison was impeccably dressed in light tan linen slacks, a linen shirt, and two-toned saddle oxfords—his customary "casual" attire for this winter resort.

In a town that was traditionally laid back and oh-so casual, Ellison's morning outfit spoke volumes about how he perceived himself or at least how he wanted to be perceived—sophisticated, civilized, cultured, even regal. It was an image he had dreamed about as a boy growing up poor in Oklahoma City in the 1920s.

In those days, his mother would bring home old copies of *Vanity Fair* magazine from her cleaning jobs in the wealthy homes of the city. Ellison devoured each issue, as much for the advertisements as for the articles, all of which exposed him to a sophisticated world—an avant-garde world beyond Oklahoma City. Years later, he would explain to an interviewer, "I wanted the world in which you wore your Sunday clothes every day. I wanted it because it represented something better, a more exciting and civilized and human way of living." To that end, Ellison saw himself and several of his friends as "young Renaissance Men, people who looked to culture and intellectualism as a source of identity."

Ellison's attire that morning in the compound was in stark contrast to his literary neighbor, the poet John Ciardi, who novelist Alison Lurie said was "more or less a slob. He always had on baggy pants and a Hawaiian shirt" —something Ellison would never own and certainly not wear.

Ellison walked the few yards to the pool, where the compound manager and resident, Tom Taylor, was speaking with the pool boy, one of many who would come and go over the years, a handsome young blond Taylor had hired to service the pool and, one can easily imagine, a few other things. Taylor was reportedly notorious for taking the pool boys under his wing and into his bed.

"Why do you always hire these young white boys to clean our pool," Ellison asked Taylor that morning. "Are you discriminating? Why don't you hire some of the black men in town?"

Taylor's smug retort was immediate. "Because," he said, "the black men in town are all doctors and lawyers and they don't want to clean our pool."

That wasn't true, of course. Not all black men in town were doctors or lawyers. But the snippy comment was, at least, somewhat reflective of how things had changed in Key West over the past century when a hundred years earlier "Key West city directories listed Black male occupations as: cigar maker, seaman, sponger, and laborer." (Black females were usually listed as seamstress or laundress.)

WHEN THIS POOL-BOY EXCHANGE OCCURRED in 1985, it had been several years since Ellison and his second wife Fanny McConnell Ellison, had bought their home on Windsor Lane, a place that Ellison described as a "dilapidated compound in the Old Town section of the island."

Charlee Wilbur had told Fanny about the compound and

Fanny thought it would be a good investment. Ralph agreed. So, on December 17, 1975, Fanny put down $1,000 on a little 960-square-foot, four-room house facing Windsor Lane and next door to the house the Herseys were buying at the same time. In March 1976, she closed on the property in her name only for $19,610.

From the beginning, Ralph and Fanny really didn't spend a great deal of time at their winter home. Ciardi, Wilbur, and Hersey were the three people who ran the compound, recalled Tom Wilson, a longtime resident. "The Ellisons were almost nonexistent. The only time I remember seeing Fanny," he said, "was at our annual association meeting in March."

Yet, on those rare visits, Ralph seemed to enjoy his environment. "The grounds which we share with our friends and neighbors are landscaped with lovely tropical plants, trees, and flowers," he once said, "though I must add that the thump of oranges and avocados on one's roof can be quite shocking."

So that morning in March of '85, after Ellison was finished admonishing the compound manager about his choice for pool maintenance, he set about trying to prune an orchid tree. Back East, Ellison found himself having to explain that orchid trees don't actually bear orchids, but they do bear lovely flowers that look like the blooms of certain orchids.

There was one problem with the orchid tree, however. As Ellison explained, he was tired of cleaning up after the bean pods that "explode button-shaped seeds with the velocity of shotgun pellets," nearly ruining the wooden deck on the front of their little house. Ellison was also frustrated with the fact that the tree "cast so much shade" it was depriving the property's beautiful flowering hibiscus plants and passion flowers from needed sunlight.

What made things worse, apparently, was the fact that the roots were encroaching into the stone wall in front of their house which provided the privacy that they cultivated as much as the orchid tree with its lovely cattleya-like blossoms.

WHEN THE ELLISONS BOUGHT into the compound in 1976, it had been almost twenty-five years since the publication of Ralph's masterpiece *Invisible Man* in 1952. His apotheosis, which had taken seven years to write, had earned him dozens of accolades and awards, including the National

Book Award in 1953—beating out two very worthy contenders: *East of Eden* by John Steinbeck and *The Old Man and the Sea* by Ernest Hemingway.

Since then, the literary world awaited his next magnum opus. But it hadn't come. Sure, there was a collection of political, social, and critical essays— *Shadow and Act*—in 1964, but the long-awaited novel was just that—awaited.

A 15-foot high Invisible Man *monument stands on Riverside Drive at 150th Street in Manhattan, honoring Ralph Ellison.*

In 1967, the Ellisons purchased (for $35,000) a 246-year-old, two-story farmhouse on Lincoln Hill Road in Plainfield, which was supposed to serve as a quiet retreat, away from their Riverside Drive apartment in Manhattan, where Ellison could write. And by October, Ralph was "writing intensely."

Their farmhouse was a quick ten-minute drive from the Ellisons' good friends, Dick and Charlee Wilbur, who owned a large, rambling home on eighty acres on Dodwells Road in Cummington. Ralph and Fanny first met Dick and Charlee Wilbur in August 1959, at the Bread Loaf writers' conference in Middlebury, Vermont, where he was scheduled to lecture as well as read manuscripts from the upcoming young writers.

The conference was founded in 1926 by a young editor named John Fararr (later the founder of a major book publishing company, Farrar and Rinehart) who believed that "new writers could be or should be helped on the road to fame by older and more established ones."

"A sense of easy intimacy quickly developed between Ralph and Dick Wilbur," said Ellison's biographer Arnold Rampersad, whose book *Ralph Ellison: A Biography* was a nonfiction finalist for the National Book Award in 2007. Their friendship developed in part, says Rampersad, because they shared the same birthday, March 1.

One can imagine Ellison and Wilbur sitting in wicker chairs on the wrap-around porch of the three-story Bread Loaf Inn, its faded yellow clapboard siding accented by dark-green shutters. While smoking a cigar and sipping a snifter of brandy, they likely discussed a variety of topics, ranging from the odd juxtaposition of poet as lyricist (Wilbur had provided the lyrics for the 1956 Broadway musical *Candide*) to the function of literature or how writing is written, two topics Ellison returned to frequently.

Soon after they bought their summer property in Plainfield, Fanny wrote to her friend Rose Styron, wife of novelist and essayist William Styron, author of *Sophie's Choice*, after reading an article in *Newsweek* magazine about the Styrons and the birth of their daughter Alexandra. According to Fanny, the article mentioned "many beautiful things" about Rose, which Fanny found very gratifying. "Every now and then," Fanny wrote, "a woman is duly credited."

Fanny also told Rose that Ralph had bought himself a tractor and had mowed acres and acres of ground "with the enthusiasm of a boy on his first bike." At the same time, they both discovered that gardening was a very peaceful hobby, which brought them a great deal of satisfaction. Twenty years later, it would be the one disappointment Ralph had about their winter home in Key West. There was no room on their property for gardening.

FROM ALL REPORTS, it was a delightful summer that summer of '67, the year the Ellisons first bought their farmhouse. The Wilburs immediately welcomed their friends to the area and introduced them to other residents, both year-round and summer.

In a letter to a friend at the time, Ellison told about the parties at the Wilburs' large, rambling home, describing his hosts as "interesting enough and humorous enough to make things swing." He continued his enthusiasm, noting, "Usually, it's black tie with a live and not too square orchestra," Ellison wrote, "and a lot of amusing academic and literary types and dam[n] good food. You have to work pretty hard at it to be bored."

The good times, however, came to a tragic and abrupt end on November 29, 1967. While Fanny and Ralph were running some errands in town that day, a fire broke out, destroying their farmhouse. The cause, according to the local fire marshal, was faulty electrical wiring. Fanny, however, never did totally buy that explanation. Years later, after

Ralph's death in 1994, Fanny expressed her long-held belief that it had been arson, motivated by racism.

While they managed to rescue their seven-year-old black Labrador retriever named Tuckatarby of Tivoli—a dog who had come into their home as a puppy with a pedigree that Ellison insisted on—they were not able to rescue Ralph's long-anticipated new novel—a novel that he had begun in Rome in 1955. How much was destroyed was never really clear. At first, Ellison suggested that he had lost most of the novel in the fire. Later, Ellison claimed he had "...a full copy of all that he had done prior to that summer." Still, later, he claimed he lost more than 360 pages.

Regardless of how much of the manuscript was destroyed, it was a devastating loss, a literary catastrophe the likes of which had not been experienced since Hemingway's first wife Hadley had packed up all his unpublished short stories to take to him in Switzerland, only to have her luggage with its precious cargo stolen at the Gare de Lyon in Paris, never to be found. Ellison later wrote about the "sheer devastation of what had been quite a lovely old house and grounds now reduced to a scene of desolation."

In March of 1968, less than four months after the blaze, Fanny promised that Ralph would deliver the manuscript "early next year." Yet, ten years later, there was still no manuscript. Fanny justified the inordinate delay by telling everyone the fire had devastated them both, making it difficult for Ralph to write. It was as if the fire had given him a legitimate excuse, however specious, for not finishing the novel.

At age eighty, a few months before his death in 1994, Ellison still maintained "there will be something very soon." But, in the end, after Ellison had died from pancreatic cancer, it was left to his close friend and literary executor, John F.

Callahan, to compile the novel from more than two thousand unorganized pages that Ellison had written over nearly forty years. The novel—*Juneteenth*—was finally published posthumously five years after Ellison's death.

SOME MIGHT SUGGEST that Ellison was destined to become a writer and that his father intentionally set him on that path when he named his young son after the eminent essayist, philosopher, and poet Ralph Waldo Emerson. Ellison would not disagree. "I came to suspect that he was aware of the suggestive powers of names and of the magic involved in naming," he would often say later in life.

In any event, when Ellison arrived in New York in 1936 on a break from his music composition studies at Tuskegee University in Alabama, his plan was to become a composer and performer of classical music. A fortuitous meeting with novelist, poet, and social activist Langston Hughes changed all that, resulting in what he called "a metamorphosis from a would-be composer to some sort of writer."

Hughes, who was thirteen years older than Ellison, was already well-known for *Not Without Laughter*, his first novel, published in 1930, and *The Ways of White Folks*, a collection of short stories published in 1934. He introduced the young, twenty-two-year-old Ellison to Richard Wright, who was just beginning to be recognized as an African-American author. (His novel *Native Son*, which focused on the oppressive effect racism had on the black population in 1930s America, would be published in 1940 and become an immediate best seller.)

Ellison had planned to go back to Tuskegee, but he and Wright hit it off and Wright encouraged Ellison to write for a new magazine called *New Challenge*. In a way, the idea seemed preposterous to Ellison; however, he soon wrote a book review and soon after that a short story. "Richard Wright took me under his wing, so to speak, and encouraged me, offering suggestions on how to tighten my writing and to structure it," Ellison said in an interview with his compound neighbor John Hersey.

In that same interview, Ellison told Hersey, how he had developed his skill as a writer. "I approached writing as I approached music," he said. "I'd been playing since I was eight years old and I knew you didn't just reach a capable performance in whatever craft without work. I'd play one set of scales over and over again. In Tuskegee I'd get up early in the morning and I'd blow sustained tones on my trumpet for an hour. I knew the other students used to hate it, but this developed embouchure, breath control. And I approached writing in the same way."

Then, in the late 1940s, Ellison met Frank Taylor, a senior editor at Reynal and Hitchcock (later absorbed by Harcourt Brace), who encouraged Ellison to work on a novel and who ultimately gave Ellison his first book contract.

It was also Taylor who was influential in getting "Battle Royal" —a story that would later become the first chapter of *Invisible Man*—published in the influential literary British magazine *Horizon: A Review of Literature and Art*. The publication of "Battle Royal" brought Ellison his first real attention from the publishing world.

In many ways, it was an odd friendship of contrasts between Ellison and Taylor. Where Taylor was flamboyant, Ellison was reserved; where Taylor was extravagant, Ellison was cautious; where Taylor was charming, Ellison was often curt. (Friends from high school remember him with a "sharp tongue" even back then.)

"Taylor had a reputation as a clever, smart publisher," said former longtime book publisher Ross Claiborne. "He was also a charmer. Everybody thought he was terrific despite his failings."

Alison Lurie agreed. "Everyone loved Frank," she said. "He was so smart and so charming. Everybody was very keen on him. We still miss him."

Taylor was also a homosexual, despite being married with four sons. His flamboyance to many people at that period of time apparently left no doubt about his true sexual orientation. As Claiborne said bluntly, "No one would have mistaken him for straight." Well, almost no one.

Ellison would later maintain that he had no idea about Taylor's preferred sexuality until 1958 when a friend told Ellison that he had been approached by Taylor "homosexually"—a fact that Ellison maintained "did nothing to lower our regard for him. Instead," Ellison said, "I resented my friend's having passed along information which I had no desire to know." In other words, "Don't Ask, Don't Tell."

Throughout his life, Ellison's attitude toward homosexuality seemed to be one of "Don't Ask, Don't Tell," the official United States policy on military service by gays, bisexuals, and lesbians instituted by the Bill Clinton administration in 1994.

(The policy, which took effect on February 28, 1994, prohibited military personnel from discriminating against or harassing homosexual or bisexual service members as long as they, essentially, remained in the closet during their time of service. Openly LGBTQ people need not apply, under the policy, which didn't end until September 20, 2011.)

The "Don't Ask, Don't Tell" policy fit Ellison's sensibilities to a T. He once commented that he didn't mind gays "as long as they didn't make it obvious." As Ellison's biographer Rampersad noted, "He was liberal, but exuberant gay culture offended him."

In the early 1960s, Taylor moved his family to Hollywood where he produced the 1961 film "The Misfits," starring Marilyn Monroe and Clark Gable. It was reportedly a fun time. In his 1969 biography, *Norma Jean: The Life and Death of Marilyn Monroe*, Fred Lawrence Guiles remarked that "to Marilyn, the Taylors were by far the liveliest and most convivial of Miller's married friends. She came, in time, to confide in both Frank and his wife Nan."

As fun as it may have been, the Taylors returned to New York after he was "threatened with blacklisting as a Hollywood liberal."

At least twice during his marriage, Taylor left his wife for a young guy, Claiborne recalled. "But then both times, after his affair was over, Nan took him back." Finally, in 1975, when Taylor was fifty-nine years old, he and Nan divorced.

Thinking back on those days, Lurie said, "It's a wonderful experience of being able to change your life, move to Key West, drop one life and take up another one," she said. "He was married, had a job in New York and four children. Then, he fell in love with the son of one of his friends, a children's book writer.

"That was probably shocking in New York, but it wasn't shocking down here," Lurie continued. "Nobody said, 'Oh, he's taken up with somebody that's 25 years younger than he is.' It didn't seem remarkable. It's very freeing not to have that kind of criticism swirling around you."

That acceptance was reflected in the fact that since at least the 1960s, if not earlier, Key West was recognized as one of the country's best-known gay and lesbian enclaves in the country—the Fire Island Pines of the South, said compound resident Tom Wilson.

The Island House on Whitehead, which may be the

longest-running men-only guesthouse in the country, opened in 1976. A few years later, in 1983, the island elected the first openly gay mayor in the state of Florida (and one of the first openly LGBTQ mayors in the U.S.)

That acceptance, some say, was also why Key West didn't have a gay pride parade until 1993, two decades after the first gay pride parades were held throughout the country in 1970. The traditional rationale or explanation was that a parade wasn't needed in a city where sexual orientation wasn't an issue. Yet, as Stephen Morris, one of the organizers of the first parade in Key West in 1993, pointed out, "It's not that it's needed; it's a celebration of being gay."

AS LIBERAL AND ACCEPTING as the island was, the issue of homosexuality played a major role in the breakup of the longtime friendship between the Wilburs and the Ellisons in the 1980s. The exact series of events leading up to the breakup between friends was complex, but began in 1983 when the Ellisons rented their home in the compound to an elderly gentleman.

Not long afterwards, the Ellisons received a letter from their tenant, saying that Frank Taylor and his companion Steve Roos (the son of the tenant and, as it was soon discovered, Taylor's paramour) wanted to replace the bed in the study.

The fact that Frank Taylor and his "lover" Steve were occupying the home was very disturbing to Ralph and Fanny. They felt they should have been told about the additional tenants in advance. The fact that they weren't told about it was "a violation of friendship and our rights as property owners," Ellison said.

As Ellison wrote in a letter to the Wilburs, ". . .being square, and holding on to certain old-fashioned notions of friendship, we would have expected our old friend Taylor to've been frank about his intentions, much as I, as a Negro, would have done had I intended to bring a white girl companion into a friend's house in a community wherein our interracial presence might have raised questions."

Matters grew decidedly worse, however, after the end of the season. The Ellisons began receiving telephone calls that were transferred to their New York number by the phone company from people who assumed that they were phoning Frank's residence. "This I took as an invasion of privacy," Ellison wrote. At that point "we were not simply at odds with an unthinking erstwhile friend, but with a half-assed trickster who seems to assume that his emergence from the closet endowed him with special privileges."

At some point during this period of time, Charlee received a letter from Fanny saying that their home had been "dirtied by Frank Taylor and his lover."

To the Wilburs, the comment was unambiguous, and word soon got around, as Ellison later wrote sardonically, that according to Dick and Charlee "the cruel Ellisons broke with Frank because they [the Ellisons] were prejudiced against homosexuals."

In protest to the allegation, Ellison wrote a six-page letter to the Wilburs insisting that neither he nor Fanny was in any way prejudiced against homosexuals, and that the charge was a baseless, if not malicious, canard. He also asserted that their longtime friendship should have provided ample evidence of that fact.

"To ascribe the break in friendship to an assumed objection on our part to Taylor's choice in lovers," Ellison wrote, ". . .is like assuming that I abhor all physicians because I lost my mother to the incompetence of a single practitioner who failed to order an X-ray after she broke her hip in a fall."

Apparently, the Wilburs had gotten wind of just how upset the Ellisons were even before receiving Ellison's letter because two weeks before Ralph had penned his discourse, Charlee had written her own letter to the Ellisons talking about "the fun we had together, the closeness, many shared experiences, both happy and painful."

She added cryptically—was it intentional? — "And everyone seems to be aware of the need for acceptance in old friends [and in] open- mindedness and forgiveness."

It was not to be, since the Ellisons still had other resentments and animosities toward the Wilburs that apparently had been festering for quite a while. Ellison expressed those resentments at the end of his lengthy letter, noting how both he and Fanny felt that the Wilburs had been pulling away from their friendship for quite a while. "When you spent a year abroad and didn't write (neither of you), I assumed that we'd reached the end of our friendship."

That seemed to put an end to it. Friendship over. Yet, Ellison's innate sense of noblesse oblige—justified or

Fanny Ellison visits the Library of Congress in 1997.

not—no doubt kept him from severing the relationship completely. He concluded his letter to the Wilburs, as any proper gentleman would, with a hint of reconciliation.

"I hope this gives you a clearer idea of our view of the matter," he wrote, "and that reading it will provide a measure of the catharsis and sense of reconciliation that I've achieved in the writing. At any rate you may take the length of it as an indication of my concern that an ultimately trivial incident could do so much damage to our friendship."

It was however, a sad conclusion to a thirty-year friendship. For the next decade, the shattered remains of the soured relationship would hang over these former friends as palpable as the Key West humidity in July. While there were pleasantries exchanged, there was never the "conscious closing-in with old friends" that Charlee had hoped for.

In 1993, a year before Ralph died of pancreatic cancer and more than a decade before Fanny passed away in 2005 at the age of ninety-three, Fanny sold the Windsor Lane home to Charles Lee for what reportedly was a nice profit.

Meanwhile, it was, perhaps, Frank Taylor who had the last word in the matter. When Taylor died in 1999 at the age of eighty-three, the *New York Times* published an obituary, including a lengthy list of authors Taylor had dealt with throughout his career—Arthur Miller, Grace Metalious, Eldridge Cleaver, Richard Wilbur, and others. The obituary, however, failed to mention Ellison. Was it simply an oversight? It's not too far-fetched to suppose that Taylor had a direct hand in the instructions he left regarding his obituary.

Ellison on Writing

"I am terribly stubborn, and once I get engaged in [a writing project], I must keep going until I finally make something out of it. I don't know what the something is going to be, but the process is one through which I make a good part of my own experience meaningful . . . in a way that creates an artifact through which I can reach other people."

~ **Ralph Ellison**

CHAPTER 3

JOHN HERSEY
The Way of a Man

Photo credit: Alison Shaw

"To be in his presence was to be in an oasis of gentleness, good humor, kindness [and] quiet pleasure in others."

— Anthony Lewis, columnist, *New York Times*

Chapter 3

JOHN HERSEY

ON SUNDAY, JANUARY 15, 1995, at 10:30 a.m., a small group of people gathered in front of a 1930 nondescript, conch-style cottage on the narrow Windsor Lane in Old Town, Key West. For nearly twenty years, the home had belonged to one of the most respected writers in American literature—Pulitzer Prize-winning author John Hersey. Now, the home was being recognized as a Literary Landmark by United for Libraries (formerly Friends of Libraries USA).

Hersey's home would join a short list of only three other Literary Landmarks in Key West at that time, including the home of poet Elizabeth Bishop on White Street and the Harry S. Truman Little White House on Front Street. (By 2018, a total of nine Literary Landmarks had been dedicated in Key West.)

Poet Richard Wilbur, Hersey's longtime friend and neighbor in the Windsor Lane compound where they both lived, unveiled the bronze plaque that would be placed on the white stucco wall in front of Hersey's house, and read the inscription in his distinctive and mellifluous voice.

Reporting death, he did not proclaim it.

To life—for all its heresy—he was open and loving.

Such pomp and circumstance that pleasant January morning under bright blue skies would clearly have embarrassed this Key West writer, author of twenty-five books over the course of more than fifty years, beginning in 1942 with his first book, *Men on Bataan*, about the heroic struggle of World War II soldiers and their leader General Douglas MacArthur in their battle to defend Bataan, a province in the Philippines, and including his journalistic tour de force, *Hiroshima*, about six survivors of the atomic bomb that the United States dropped on Hiroshima, Japan, on the morning of August 6, 1945."

The Herseys' house on Windsor Lane. The bronze plaque designating the house as a Literary Landmark is to the right of the front gate.

Of all the artists I've known," Wilbur told the small group at the dedication ceremony that morning, "John was the most sincerely adverse to publicity. He would have been alarmed to see us all flocked here in front of his house."

Barbara Hersey, his wife of thirty-four years, agreed. "He was very shy of publicity," she said. (In fact, Hersey didn't give his first interview until 1984, nearly forty years after the publication of *Hiroshima*.) "But he would be both honored and over- whelmed by this, as I am."

Ed Block, a Key West friend joked about how low-key Hersey was com- pared to Wilbur. "With Hersey," Block said, "you could go into a restaurant and never know he was there. But Wilbur was a performer. When he was in a room, you knew it, not in a braggadocio way but his presence was always apparent."

After the brief ceremony, the group walked the short distance to the Key West Library on Fleming, where there was a reception in the Palm Garden, and where Hersey's friends reminisced and shared memories of their distinguished friend. Words like loyal and elegant and brilliant floated freely throughout the garden.

Two years earlier, at a memorial service for Hersey on Martha's Vineyard, where the Herseys had a summer home, novelist, and friend Peter Feibleman, author of the 1958 critically acclaimed novel *A Place Without Twilight*, talked about Hersey's dry (and sometimes dark) sense of humor.

Once, when visiting the Herseys, Peter was feeling, as he put it, "down in the mouth and limp," which of course Hersey noticed. So, he sat down next to Peter and asked him what was wrong.

"I told him about how four of my friends had died over a relatively short period of time, and about how bereft and sad I felt. And Hersey said, softly, 'Would you rather go with them, Peter?'"

Dick Reynolds, a neighbor in the Windsor Lane compound who had known both Barbara and John Hersey since he moved into the compound from New York City in

1984, remembered Hersey this way. "He was a New England-bred Atticus Finch, plain and simple."

The analogy to Finch—arguably one of the most modest and most humble characters in American literature—perfectly personified a man who was measured, studied, calm, a bit formal, perhaps, but a true gentleman.

"Hersey could be very formal with people he didn't know," said the somewhat formal Alison Lurie, "much more so than Wilbur. But in a way he had to be. So many people wanted to talk to him, to get him to write for them. So, he had to protect himself more than Dick. It was easier for Dick to be anonymous."

And, by all accounts, it was in Key West and in this secluded residential compound that Hersey could be the most anonymous. "For John," Dick Reynolds said, "the compound was an enormously pleasing oasis."

HERSEY WAS SIXTY YEARS OLD when he and his second wife, Barbara, bought their modest two-bedroom, one bath, 930-square-foot Key West cottage in the Windsor Lane compound. Their home was to the right of the double gates that opened to the lush, tropical garden-like setting.

The Herseys purchased their cottage more than thirty years after Hersey had won a Pulitzer Prize for Fiction for his third novel, *A Bell for Adano*, about "an Italian-American major in World War II who wins the love and admiration of the local townspeople when he searches for a replacement for the 700-year-old town bell that had been melted down for bullets by the fascists."

At the compound, Hersey kept a rigorous work schedule, as he did at his home "up north" in Fairfield, Connecticut, where he had a small book-lined writing studio a short distance from the main house, or at his summer home in the community of Vineyard Haven on Martha's Vineyard. There, his second-floor study "afforded a spectacular view across Vineyard Haven Harbor" where ferries running to and from the mainland passed in front of his window.

"He was very regular in his habits," recalled Baird, one of Hersey's sons with his first wife. "Every morning he would write, in longhand, double-spaced, so that he could make corrections. In the afternoons he would answer correspondence. He got lots of mail, and there was only one kind of letter he would not answer. If the name was spelled 'Hershey,' it went in the trash can."

At the compound, Hersey's writing schedule was no less rigorous or rigid. "You could set your watch by him," said Judith Daykin, whose own home in the compound, which was originally owned by John and Judith Ciardi, was almost within touching distance of Hersey's writing studio.

"Each morning, at precisely 9:00 a.m.," Daykin said, "Hersey would come out the back door of his home and follow the path around the pool to his studio. The front door to the studio was a metal door with louvers. And you'd hear it clang as he opened it. He'd write 'til twelve noon on the dot. Then you'd hear the door clang once again as he left to walk the short distance to his house where Barbara would have lunch waiting for him. He would then return to the studio at 1:00 p.m., door clanging once more to alert you to the time, and he would write until 5:00. Clang."

After work, local residents would often see a very distinguished- looking gentleman riding his bike among the equally distinguished-looking Victorian and Bahamian homes with their unique wooden decorations known as gingerbread, or perhaps returning from Fausto's grocery store on Simonton, a six-pack of Beck's beer (his favorite) in the bike's basket.

"His passion was fishing," said Ed Block, "which he did at his home on Martha's Vineyard where he kept a boat docked in front of their Vineyard Haven house and here. I could never get him to talk about his book *Hiroshima*," he said, "but if I asked him about fishhooks, I'd get a discourse."

IN FEBRUARY 1988, RANDOM HOUSE released the paperback edition of John Hersey's twenty-first book, *Blues*, a story ostensibly about a conversation between a fisherman and a stranger as they spend the summer together fishing for blues, large-mouth aggressive fish that were known to lunge at and bite careless anglers. But, of course, the book was about much more. As *The New Yorker* magazine explained in its review, the book is about "the ties between mankind and the natural world, among others."

For the narrative, Hersey had drawn on his knowledge and experiences catching this fish off the coast of Martha's Vineyard and in Key West. Like Hersey's own travel schedule, the bluefish would range off the coast of Florida during the winter months and then head north to Massachusetts before April, returning south again in October.

Appended to each chapter of *Blues* are recipes for preparing bluefish and poems from an assortment of Hersey's poet friends, including one 1978 poem by John Ciardi called "The Lung Fish," which includes the memorable line—a line one could easily imagine that Ciardi had written about himself.

"If no creature is mortal,

some are more stubborn than others."

Soon after the publication of the paperback edition of *Blues*, Hersey and his wife Barbara invited Tom Taylor, the resident manager of the compound, and Taylor's business partner, Charles Lee, to dinner at their Key West home. In honor of the publication of the paperback edition, Hersey planned to broil bluefish.

The fact that Hersey was Chef de Cuisine that night for a fish he had caught would surprise no one, since he was known to be as skilled in cooking fish as he was in catching them. "Hersey was not only a skilled fisherman," Block said, "but a skilled cook. He once taught my wife the proper way to cook yellowtail snapper."

In all likelihood, he broiled the bluefish that night, as he had so many other nights, by coating the fillet "with a glaze made by mixing minced, sautéed scallions and ginger with mayonnaise and soy sauce."

As Tom Taylor and Charles Lee walked the short distance that night from Tom's house at the rear of the compound, around the pool, and to the back door of the Herseys' house, Charles was nervous. "We should have read the book," he told Tom. For a brief moment, Charles thought maybe he could just say he had read it and hope there would be no further discussion. But then he quickly realized he would probably get caught in a "fish story" and he didn't want to obfuscate the truth as he had done a couple years earlier.

In that situation, Hersey had just published *The Call*, a novel told in the form of a fictional biography about a New York farm boy who becomes a missionary in China, a scenario very familiar to Hersey who was born in China where his parents were missionaries. (Chinese was his first language.)

Both Lee and Taylor had tried to read the seven-hundred-page tome, but they had gotten bored before a third of the way through. "We thought it was awful," Lee admitted. "We couldn't understand it. So, we hid from Hersey for a while after it came out, afraid he was going to ask us if we had read it or what we thought."

"Hi, come on in." It was Barbara at the backdoor, drink in hand—the first of her customary two drinks per evening. Barbara loved men, gay or straight. She dressed for them, Charles once said. And, as usual, she looked lovely, casual for a pleasant Key West evening. John joined them immediately, dressed, in his customary tweed sports jacket with leather elbow patches.

If Herseys' guests that evening had expected the dinner to be formal and stuffy, given the stature of their esteemed host, it was by all accounts, anything but. "Like always," Lee said, "Hersey was very easy to talk with. You would never know he was a distinguished literary figure."

In the end, Lee couldn't remember precisely what they talked about that evening—maybe it was about the Winter Olympics in Calgary, Canada, that were concluding that week, or maybe it was the Black Monday stock market crash from the previous October, a topic that still had people reeling. Or maybe the conversation centered around the easy free-flowing life of Key West. He didn't remember.

What Lee did remember, however, was that it was a delightful evening, with a perfectly delicious bluefish for dinner.

IN 1958, JOHN HERSEY and his first wife, Frances Ann Cannon, divorced and Hersey married Barbara Day Addams Kaufman, the ex-wife of the American cartoonist Charles Addams and reportedly the model for Morticia Addams, the fictional character from *The Addams Family* television series. (Morticia first appeared in Charles Addams' sinister newspaper cartoons.)

"Barbara was a beautiful lady," said Billy Cauthen, the young man who through serendipity got a part-time job in the compound when he first arrived in Key West, and, more than a quarter of a century later, was still there as a maintenance manager, construction supervisor, and overall good friend to all of the residents. "She also had a wonderful sense of humor."

As Barbara got older, she developed arthritis which got quite bad over time. "She had difficulty walking," recalled Cauthen. "The bottom of her feet were just open sores, and the doctors thought they might have to amputate her legs."

But Barbara in her own humorous way flatly objected. "Oh, no, they can't do that," Cauthen recalled her saying with a chuckle. "I'm too short as it is."

"Barbara was lovely," said Alison Lurie. "She was always so sweet; so kind to everybody. So much fun. She knew everybody. We all loved her."

Mangoes restaurant on Duval and Angela.

During the winter season in Key West, Barbara and her friends frequently visited Mangoes for lunch, a restaurant on the corner of Duval and Angela where Barbara's favorite table at the railing next to the sidewalk on Duval was always waiting for her. "The co-owner of Mangoes at the time, Amy Culver, was very fond of Barbara, as was the head waiter," said Dick Reynolds. "As Barbara's hands became more arthritic, they would cut up her entree, thus enabling Barbara's arthritic hands to work to full advantage."

After Barbara died in 2007 at the age of eighty-eight, her

daughter Brook held a memorial reception for Barbara's many friends at Mangoes. But as the result of a misunderstanding, the bar was charging guests for their drinks. "When I told Brook about this," said Reynolds, "she asked if I would immediately let the bartenders know not to charge anyone. 'Mother would be appalled,' she said."

David Wolkowsky with Barbara Hersey.

Throughout their years in Key West, the Herseys maintained friendships with many other literary figures who had homes on the island, including poet and literary critic John Malcolm Brinnin, author of *Dylan Thomas in America: An Intimate Journey.* (Brinnin had brought the alcoholic "Do not go gentle into that good night" poet to the U.S. from Wales in 1949 and befriended him until Thomas's death in 1953 at the age of thirty-nine.)

According to Reynolds, Brinnin had a glorious apartment overlooking the water. But he felt sorry for his good friend Barbara. "He felt she was living in squalor in our little compound," Dick said, obviously amused by the recollection. "He thought the compound was beneath her."

"So, when Brinnin died in 1998, five years after John Hersey's death, he left this very grand apartment to Barbara," Reynolds recalled, "thinking she deserved better and assuming she would be delighted to take up residence in a place far more suited to her station in life."

How wrong he was!

"Barbara very gamely went down there to try it out," Reynold recalled, "but she spent only one season there. That was enough for her. 'They're too uppity for me down there,' she said."

So, according to Reynolds, she came back to her friends in the compound where she felt comfortable. "Everybody in the compound looked out for her and loved her," Reynolds said. "She had long ago found a home, not only in Key West, but in our little compound on Windsor Lane."

AT THE COMPOUND there was—at least for a while—a genuine camaraderie among Hersey, Richard Wilbur, and John Ciardi. "You had the sense it was like they were the oldest of school buddies," said compound resident Tom Wilson. That was true, perhaps, but no more so than when they were playing their weekly two-hour game of anagrams.

Anagrams is a fascinating and challenging word game, so it should come as no surprise that these men—all of whom loved the intricate and intriguing lexicon of the English language—were avid game players.

The game sounds simple enough: start with one word and form a new word, either by rearranging letters (bat to tab, for example) or by adding one or two additional letters (bat to bait), keeping in mind that the competition can steal a player's word by adding at least one letter to make a new word. Whoever gets eight words first, wins. Easy, right?

But with philologists like Hersey, Ciardi, and Wilbur—not to mention visiting players who often added their own temperament and idiosyncratic playing styles to the game, such as Leonard Bernstein who was notorious for playing out of turn—it's easy to understand how the games would often turn into what John Malcolm Brinnin called "socially acceptable mayhem."

Each player had his own specialty when it came to the manipulation of words. Hersey was an expert on nautical terms. He "knew all the names of all the fish in the sea and he was very good at any word connected with boats and fishing."

Hersey's ability to use the right word for any occasion was legend. At his memorial service, Brook Hersey told how her father once described a character as having a "massive, *pyknic* build," not to impress anyone with his use of the English language, but because it was the absolutely perfect word to describe the man who had "a thick neck, large abdomen, and relatively short legs."

A year after Hersey's death, Alfred A. Knopf, Hersey's publisher for more than twenty years, released *Key West Tales*, the last book Hersey finished six weeks before his death. The book consists of fifteen short stories set in Key West, one of which is called "A Game of Anagrams."

The four anagram players in the short story are only thinly disguised fictional characters for the real-life anagram players at the compound. (Wilbur claimed he was Forrester in the story, while Hersey's description of the fictional player Paladin—a 280-pound lexicographer who had published many slim volumes of poetry and "three dictionaries, one of Elizabethan English, one of Midwestern U.S. slang, and one of words with seven letters" —was easily recognized by even the most casual reader as Ciardi.)

In Hersey's story, the four players show their amazing skill at the game, much in the way a real game was played at the compound. Chalker [Hersey in real life] grabs HEAL and adds the letter C to make it LEACH, while Paladin steals LEACH and adds two letters to make CHOLERA and

Forester who holds the letter B "takes his time transforming the dread disease into BACHELOR."

Hersey would frequently dominate the game, even after he had had a stroke, according to Wilbur. But after Hersey's death, the game became "dormant," Brinnin said "We didn't play much last spring without John. We just couldn't face it."

THERE WAS, PERHAPS, ONLY ONE blemish on Hersey's character throughout his life. In 1988, when Hersey was seventy-four years old, he was accused of breaking the Golden Rule of journalism— "Thou shall not copy someone else's work as your own." The plagiarism charge had to do with an essay he wrote for *The New Yorker* about novelist James Agee. There were, as it was later discovered, similarities in his essay published in *The New Yorker* July 18, 1988 to passages from *James Agee: A Life*, a biography written by Laurence Bergreen in 1984.

For Hersey to be charged with something as journalistically repugnant as plagiarism was almost unimaginable. Yet, it was apparently true, since he subsequently apologized for "appropriating another writer's facts and phrases without attribution" noting in a gentlemanly fashion that he regretted any "discourtesy" or "distress" caused to Mr. Bergreen.

Yet, his admission seemed halfhearted, perfunctory, insincere. In a way it was like Arthur Dimmesdale apologizing to his Puritan congregation for unspecified transgressions without acknowledging the true nature of those transgressions, but with one big difference. Dimmesdale was truly anguished by what he viewed were his sins, whereas one never had the feeling that Hersey truly believed his "appropriation of facts and phrases" was that big a deal. In any event, in Hersey's mind, it certainly didn't rise to the level of plagiarism. "I don't believe my real offense in terms of normal practice is great," Hersey said. "There's always been a fine line between facts and the work of another writer."

Those who knew Hersey—both friends and former students—were stunned at the reports. No one could believe the allegation could be true about a man who treasured the written word.

"This sounded nothing like the teacher we had in class, and it was something I never understood," a former student told the *Washington Post*. Friends and colleagues could not have agreed more.

WHEN HERSEY DIED IN 1993, Hendrick Hertzberg, senior editor at *The New Yorker*, wrote an obituary for the magazine, calling Hersey's *Hiroshima* his "crowning achievement." The thirty-one-thousand-word story was first published in its entirety in the August 31, 1946, issue of *The New Yorker*. Never before, nor since, had the magazine devoted its entire editorial space in a single issue to one article— "no Talk of the Town, no cartoons, no reviews."

As Hertzberg wrote in the obituary, "Hersey's reporting was so meticulous, his sentences and paragraphs were so clear, calm, and restrained, that the horror of the story he had to tell came through all the more chillingly."

The horror of the story as Hersey told it affected millions of people around the world, including one sixth grader who later in life became a writer himself, publishing eight novels, while holding a variety of writer-in-waiting jobs along the way, not the least of which was "a general of the Egyptian army" or as he explains, "a non-singing role in the New York City Opera's production of Handel's *Julius Caesar.*" That writer was Edward Hower, husband of Alison Lurie.

"Our teacher, the only liberal in our community, gave us a copy of *Hiroshima* which absolutely scarred me for life," Hower said. "I've been a lifelong pacifist ever since. I even refused to join the army during the Vietnam War."

In addition to Hersey's memorable novels, the 6-foot-2-inch-tall, ruggedly handsome litterateur taught two writing courses in fiction and nonfiction at Yale University in New Haven, CT, over the course of eighteen years. "He was the type of person who would study relentlessly the photos of an incoming class so that he could greet each one by name," his daughter Brook said.

Often, he urged his students in his fiction-writing seminar to study the story-telling techniques and descriptive prose of Ralph Ellison's novel *Invisible Man*, one of Hersey's favorite books. (Besides being a neighbor in the compound, Ellison was also a longtime good friend of Hersey's.)

While he enjoyed teaching, writing always remained Hersey's first passion. As he told a reporter when he retired from Yale in 1984, "If I weren't writing a book, I wouldn't know myself."

When asked which one of his own books was his favorite, however, Hersey—a gentleman and a diplomat—responded as one would expect. "I have five kids and if you asked me which one was my favorite, I wouldn't tell you, even if I had one, and neither would I tell you if I had a favorite book."

HERSEY DIED OF A STROKE at 2:45 a.m. on March 25, 1993, although he also had colon and liver cancer. His wife Barbara, and his family (including his five children) were by his side at his home on Windsor Lane.

Three months later, on June 19, 1993, there was a memorial service for Hersey on Martha's Vineyard "at the tiny white-fenced cemetery on the road from Vineyard

Haven to the end of West Chop" on the north end of the island, the same cemetery where William Styron was also buried when he died in 2006.

People came from all over came to honor their distinguished friend, including many of his Key West friends—John Malcolm Brinnin, poet James Merrill and his partner David Jackson, Richard and Charlee Wilbur, and David Wolkowsky, among them.

"It was an occasion of celebration," Wolkowsky said, one that included graveside tributes and a marching jazz band, "much like those John had watched passing his Windsor Lane home near the local cemetery."

Those traditional African-American jazz funerals that Hersey had certainly observed would always start with the faint sound of a drum, muffled at first, over on Elizabeth. But then the sound grew steadily louder in cadence with the deep low thump-thump beat of the tuba, as the full marching brass band made the turn at the top of Elizabeth and Windsor. The procession, headed by women mourners dressed all in white, men in black suits, would sway from side to side in tempo with the somber dirge, as the procession moved toward the historic Key West cemetery at the foot of Windsor, where more than a hundred thousand souls rest in peace, an amazing number for an island with a population of only about twenty-seven thousand. The procession was a tradition many African-Americans had followed ever since they arrived in Key West in the early 1800s from the Bahamas.

Of the many tributes that day on Martha's Vineyard, Peter Feibleman's words perhaps best summed up the character of the man so many had come to know and respect. Feibleman recalled how totally impressed he was with Hersey when they first met. "I remember thinking, 'So that's what a man is.' Something about the way he moved, spoke, sat still—

something about the way he held himself: John's way was the way of a man."

Hersey's daughter Brook told the friends who had gathered there that day that she had spoken to her father shortly before he died. Like a Buddhist, who believes that a peaceful state of mind is important when one dies if he or she is to find a happy state of rebirth, her father wanted to know only about one thing—a white hibiscus. "In dying," Brook said, "he wanted to know that a flower he'd planted was thriving and that it was beautiful."

It was.

John Hersey on Writing

"To be a writer is to sit down at one's desk in the chill portion of every day, and to write; not waiting for the little jet of the blue flame of genius to start from the breastbone - just plain going at it, in pain and delight. To be a writer is to throw away a great deal, not to be satisfied, to type again, and then again, and once more, and over and over."

~ **John Hersey**

RICHARD WILBUR
A Good and Decent Man

Photo courtesy of Arlo Haskell

"Courtly, courteous, and civilized: he showed a lot of
us how to live as both a person and as a poet."

-- Poet R.S. "Sam" Gwynn

Chapter 4

RICHARD WILBUR

THERE'S A STORY that poet Richard (Dick) Wilbur told frequently throughout the last forty years of his life. It was a story that had many iterations over the years, but basically recounted how he and his wife Charlee were first introduced to Key West.

It was the 1960s, and a colleague of Dick's asked him, "Why do you take winter vacations in remote places like Tobago, using up all your money on airfare? You ought to try Key West, our American subtropics."

So, Dick asked, "Well, what's it like?"

And the friend thought for a moment and then asked: "Have you ever seen the movie *Bonnie and Clyde* with its mixture of beauty and tawdriness?"

"Well, yes," Dick replied. "We thought it was morally questionable, but, aesthetically, very pleasing."

"Great," the friend replied. "Then you'll love Key West."

And, so, off they went that winter to give Key West a try, renting a room at the Sun 'N Surf Motel on South Street near Duval, the southernmost motel in the continental U.S. at the time.

"I remember when we settled in, we sat out on the balcony in the heat and realized we were going to require a drink, something with tonic," Dick recalled. "So, I went out and trudged all over town for tonic water, but I couldn't find any and had to settle for Tom Collins mix."

"'No tonic?' Charlee asked when I returned. I shook my head no."

"Well, thank God," she said. "We've found a backwater."

In March 1976, that backwater town—Key West—became their permanent winter retreat. "The great thing about Key West," Dick would say years later, "the thing we loved most was that it was an island full of an extraordinary variety of people. It was about 45% Cuban, about 8% island blacks . . . and retired Navy people and active Navy people as well, people devoted to fishing, people devoted to sailing, lots of gay people. All these very different people were tolerant of each other. That gave the island extraordinary charm. What people did about the difference was to laugh at it or laugh with it and laugh in a not unkind manner."

For nearly three decades—from 1976 until 2005 when Charlee became too ill to travel—they spent at least three months each winter with this "extraordinary variety of people" in a tropical paradise they called home.

IN HIS JUNIOR YEAR at Amherst College, Amherst, MA—the alma mater of many poets, including James Merrill who would years later become Wilbur's Key West neighbor—Dick Wilbur met the love of his life—Charlotte (Charlee) Hayes Ward, a sophomore at nearby Smith College. They met on a blind date. "In those days," Dick explained, "it was believed that if you could just find the right girl, everything was going to be all right, and I believed that."

Dick and Charlee on their wedding day.

Charlee personified everything that Dick had ever hoped for in a wife and partner. She was beautiful, talented, smart. It was true love from the start—the kind of "True Love" that Bing Crosby sang about to Grace Kelly in the 1956 movie *High Society*.

Fortunately, Charlee came from a literary background. She was the granddaughter of the first person to publish a poem by Robert Frost in his magazine *The Independent*, a highly respected literary magazine at the time. As a result, Frost would later refer to Charlee's grandfather as "the first friend of my poetry."

Coming from such literary lineage, it's not surprising that as a young girl Charlee felt that one day she would marry a poet. But she had one requirement. His name had to be Richard. "I was absolutely addled with love of Richard the Lion-Hearted at the time," she said. So, when she met poet Richard Wilbur in 1941, it was, for her, kismet.

For his part, it was as close to love at first sight as one can get. "I felt happy to be with Charlee right away," Dick said, "and had no wish to leave her." And as soon as Charlee graduated from Smith in 1942, they were married.

Willa Muir, the wife of the Scottish poet and novelist Edwin Muir, once told Richard Wilbur that his wife, Charlee, was "the perfect poet's wife. It was a life she seemed almost destined to live."

Years later, those who knew Charlee at the compound would agree. "Charlee was the driving force behind Dick," compound manager Charles Lee said. "She was his agent, publicist, right arm. Charlee shielded him, so he was able to write with no interference. She took care of finances."

Dick described her influence on him a different way. "Charlee, without being at all coercive, civilized me," he said.

For nearly sixty-five years, the two were inseparable. They had a devoted, trusting relationship, a remarkable bond that was perhaps no better exemplified than by a situation that occurred shortly after their marriage, when Dick was stationed in France during the war.

While there, he met a woman—certainly not surprising for G.I.s overseas during the war. But for some reason, someone—no one ever knew who—took it upon himself (herself?) to send an innocuous photo of Dick and the young woman to Charlee, suggesting alleged infidelity.

Wilbur discovered that the picture had been sent to his bride and immediately sent her a message alerting her to the fact that this so-called scandalous picture would be forthcoming. He also sent her a bottle of her favorite perfume.

According to Wilbur's biographers, Robert and Mary Bagg, the photo and the bottle of perfume were enough evidence to support an alleged affair.

Yet, to Charlee whether there was or wasn't a liaison in France really wasn't the point. She knew their devotion and commitment to each other was never in doubt and she made that perfectly clear in a touching (and even humorous) response to him—a response (reported in the Baggs' biography) that expressed their love more poignantly and powerfully than all the romantic Hallmark cards in the world.

> You're a dolt! Did you really think you had to forewarn me about that picture of you and that sexy-looking French Frail? Even if I saw a picture of you actually in bed with such a babe, I shouldn't think any other thought than—"god, I'd like to be in her shoes!" (Or out of them as the case might be.) You must remember that I have tremendous respect for your essential *taste*.

And I also have great faith in and dependence upon our common love so that whatever you did couldn't possibly touch the good that ties us irrevocably together.

As Dick would say throughout their many years together, "I was terribly lucky that she decided I would do."

IN 1947, WHEN WILBUR was only twenty-six years old, Reynal & Hitchcock (the same publisher who had encouraged Ralph Ellison early in his career) published Wilbur's first book of poetry *The Beautiful Changes and Other Poems*. It received excellent reviews, and immediately identified him as a poet of "outstanding perception."

Over the next half century, Wilbur published eleven other books of poetry, two of which received the Pulitzer Prize for Poetry, one in 1957, the other in 1989; he wrote many children's verses, and translated many riddles by Symphosius, who wrote in the late fourth or early fifth century; he provided the original lyrics for the Lillian Hellman/Leonard Bernstein production of Voltaire's *Candide* in 1956, and translated many French playwrights, including the comedies of Molière and the dramas of Racine; he also translated the poetry of Russian and Italian poets—something he used to do "for fun."

"When I don't have notions for my own poems, often I'll work on a translation," he said. "It's easier than writing something uncalled for."

He also confessed in his own humorous way, "I almost always have some translation project going to keep me busy in between visits from the muse."

During that time, he also taught English at Wesleyan University for twenty years and assumed the position of writer-in-residence at Smith College until 1986.

BY THE TIME THE WILBURS were in their mid-thirties, everything seemed perfect in their lives. Wilbur had won the 1957 Pulitzer Prize in Poetry for his collection *Things of This World: Poems* (published in 1956), had received the first of many honorary doctorates, and had translated a successful production of Molière's *Le Misanthrope* playing at Theatre East in Manhattan.

They were a popular couple, a devoted couple, an attractive couple, a Tracey/Hepburn couple of the literary world. Wherever they went, whether it was a cocktail party or an academic event, people wanted to be around them, to talk with them, to be seen with them.

"We were always being told that we were beautiful, gifted, star-touched," said Charlee, as she reflected on earlier years in a *People* magazine interview in 1987. "Everything that Dick applied for he seemed to get, and if he didn't apply, they came to him anyway. I was told that I was the best hostess, the best housekeeper, the best financial manager, the best mother, you name it," Charlee said. "It almost seemed like fate that something bad would happen."

So, when it was discovered that their fourth child, Aaron, had autism—today known as autism spectrum disorder (ASD), which has to do with a group of complex neurodevelopment disorders—Charlee took the diagnosis stoically, but was resolute in her determination to learn as much about the disorder and what could be done to help her son as possible. And over several years, she became quite knowledgeable on the subject.

"Charlee was a very strong, independent woman," said Dick Reynolds, a longtime compound resident and friend of the Wilburs. "So, it's not surprising that she would have immediately set about learning everything she could about this unfamiliar disorder and how to help their son."

Later, Charlee wanted to share her knowledge and experience about autism with other parents with autistic children. So, she had

Dick and Charlee Wilbur at a cocktail party in Key West.

business cards printed listing herself as "freelance counselor in genetic chemical imbalances"—a title some in the compound found mildly amusing if not misrepresentative since she had no formal training or credentials in the subject "other than the business cards she printed herself," said one compound resident.

After seven years, according to Dick, Aaron's condition lifted, leaving him learning disabled but, "capable of keeping a checkbook and holding a job in a restaurant. He has a girl and takes her out for beers."

Later on in life, both Charlee and Dick combatted a serious drug addiction problem. While working in France, both became addicted to Valium, a drug they took initially just to help them sleep but which soon led to behavioral effects similar to alcohol addiction.

After returning to the U.S., they tried to get off the drug which was much more difficult than they had imagined. "We were suddenly climbing the walls," Wilbur recalled. "And to be brief about it, I found myself in a locked ward at one point because I was so depressed. And my wife's condition was scarcely better. It took us quite a while to get over that quite innocent addiction."

But unlike so many of his fellow poets at the time who let drugs and depression destroy their lives—Sylvia Plath, for one, who at age thirty famously put her head in the oven and turned on the gas—Wilbur overcame his own addiction.

"I had the luck to be very happily married, and so there was always a central calm and joy in my life. I think that helped me not go the self-destructive ways of some of my friends. Although I also think I must have an iron stomach because when all that drinking was being done, I did quite a lot myself."

"I DIDN'T KNOW WHO THESE PEOPLE WERE when I first started working at the compound," said Billy Cauthen. "I certainly had no idea that Dick was a famous poet. Dick and all of the other writers who lived in the compound were just ordinary people to me."

Over the next quarter century, Billy and the Wilburs became particularly close. "They were a wonderful couple," Cauthen said, "extremely caring for each other." And, he might have added, from all accounts, extremely passionate and without any Puritan modesty.

Often, when doing some work for the Wilburs, Cauthen would go to their home in the compound early in the morning and knock on their door.

"Who is it, Charlee?" he'd hear Dick yell out in a basso profundo voice worthy of Mufasa, the character in Disney's *The Lion King* voiced by James Earl Jones.

"Hold on," Charlee would reply as she peeked out the window. "Oh, it's only Billy," she'd say. Then, opening the door, she'd add, "Come on in, Billy."

And so, in he'd go and much to Cauthen's surprise—at least at first—they'd both be totally nude. Then, Charlee would say to their friend, "Go ahead and do what you need to do today, Billy." According to Cauthen, "It didn't ever bother them that I was there, and they were nude. They were that unassuming and casual."

"Unassuming" is a word used a lot by people who knew Dick. Tom Wilson, a longtime compound resident, told how he once asked Dick to sign one of his books, which he did quite willingly. "But after he signed it," Wilson said, "he realized he had written 'Richard Wilbur' and immediately apologized. 'I didn't mean to sign it Richard,' he said. 'I should have just signed it Dick.'"

"That's how down to earth and unpretentious he was," Wilson said. "He was also a true gentleman."

ONE SPRING DAY IN 1984, Dick was in the compound washing his car. He had parked the car on the narrow brick path—almost too narrow for a car, really—that led from the front gate past the pool to John Ciardi's house, the only house that was *in* the compound but not *part of* the compound. The path separated the back of the Wilbur home, now a two-story structure, with the pool.

The garden hose was on the ground, water running down the brick path where it pooled in a little puddle around the front double-wide gate on Windsor. Wilbur—tall, robust, now more mature looking at sixty-three years old than the youthful, boyish-looking young man in his wedding-day photo—made broad soapy circular motions around the hood of the car. It was clear he wore his late middle age well, looking at least ten years younger than the truth.

Some classical music, almost inaudible, could be heard from a window at the rear of the house facing the brick path and the car wash. The fresh beguiling aroma of damp gum leaf oils filled the air.

Suddenly, a stranger in tan khaki pants, white polo shirt, and tangerine-tinted glasses pushed open the gate, stepped over the muddy pool of water, and waved hello to Dick.

When Wilbur saw the stranger, he walked over to the back of his house to turn off the running water, wiped his hands on his pants, and then as the stranger approached, Wilbur stretched out his hand.

"Good morning," Wilbur said. A feral cat, one of many in the compound, dashed across the brick path to a bougainvillea where it turned, sat, and eyed the stranger suspiciously.

It was at that moment that the two men realized they knew each other, but from where? Had they met at one of the endless cocktail parties in Key West this season? Or was it longer ago?

"Dick," the stranger said, with an expression of surprise, realizing he knew the gentleman car-washer. "John Price here." Thirty years earlier, Price had invested in *Candide*. It was then the two had met.

The reunion that spring morning in 1984 was so unexpected and so enthusiastic that Price forgot that Judith Daykin, his longtime partner, was sitting in the car on Windsor Lane, waiting for him.

"I'm sitting there, waiting and waiting and waiting," Judith recalled, "and thinking 'What the hell is he doing in there.'"

Meanwhile, Price explained to his old acquaintance that he and Judith had come to the compound that day because they heard there was a house for sale in this hidden enclave and they were looking for a winter retreat. But when they got to the gated compound, Judith felt uneasy about going in without a real estate agent, so she decided to wait in the car while John went in to "peek around" the property.

"Nonsense," Wilbur said. "Go tell her to come on in. I'll take you back to the house that's for sale. It's rented right now, but you can peek in the windows. There's no one home."

Once reunited, John and Judith went back into the compound, where Wilbur led them down the path, around the pool, and past another small structure—John Hersey's writing studio, they were told—to the tiny cigar-maker's cottage that was for sale, one of the homes in the compound formerly owned by poet John Ciardi.

They couldn't get into the house that day, but were immediately attracted to what they saw as they peeked in the windows. A short narrow hallway led to the back of the house and the kitchen. To the right of the front door was a small bedroom hardly big enough for a queen-size bed. Behind that room was an even smaller room that Ciardi (like other owners that followed) used as his office. To the left of the hallway was another small room that was the living room, which led to an outside porch (which was later enclosed to make a large dining room). Every room was painted Caribbean blue.

It appeared to both Price and Daykin that the house needed work. There was deferred maintenance, for sure. But they loved it. The good thing was that the home was constructed of Dade County pine—a strong, durable wood that they would later learn was highly resistant to decay and insect damage. (It once grew between the Everglades and the Atlantic in South Florida, but today has been almost completely harvested and no longer available.)

"We loved the fact that it was tucked way back in the

compound away from the pool," Daykin said, "with a tiny deck and a big avocado tree outside." By May, they closed on the sale of the house. They were now owners of a tiny little corner of paradise in a compound on an island paradise.

OVER THE YEARS, Price and Daykin became good friends with the Wilburs. "We were on their wavelength," Daykin said. "We had an immediate affinity with them in part because of our show business background."

Daykin had made a name for herself as an arts administrator, first as the manager of the Paul Taylor Dance Company in the 60s, then Executive VP of the Brooklyn Academy of Music (BAM). (Later, in 1992, she would assume the position of President, CEO, and founder of New York City Center's *Encores! Great American Musicals in Concert* productions, a concert series dedicated to performing rarely heard American musicals which was launched in 1994 with three musicals: Fiorello!, Allegro, and Lady in the Dark. (Daykin retired in 2003, having trans- formed City Center into a performing arts powerhouse.)

John Price and Judith Daykin in Key West soon after buying their home in the compound in 1984.

Price was the founder of Musicarnival in Warrensville, OH, a popular theater-in-the-round that produced dozens of Broadway musicals for more than twenty years. He was originally a weather forecaster, known as "Mr. Weather-Eye," for a local TV station in Cleveland, but he had a dream. He imagined a summer theater-in-the- round under a huge Barnum and Bailey-like tent over a circular stage. When he talked about his vision back then, you could almost hear Andy Hardy exclaiming in his 1939 movie *Babes in Arms,* "I know, we'll put on a show."

Price had decided to launch his dream in a suburban setting in Warrensville Heights, OH, a stone's throw from Thistledown Race Track. While other young Navy veterans like himself might have been thinking about putting their money on the horses at Thistledown, Price envisioned putting his money on something more spectacular than what could be found on a one-mile oval dirt track. He envisioned "chorus girls breaking into routines just beyond the oval rail" of the theater, and musical productions set right in the middle of his audience in the round.

And in 1954, Price launched his dream with a production of Rogers and Hammerstein's *Oklahoma!* On opening night, he ran down the aisle from the back of the new theater—something he would do hundreds of times over the next twenty-plus years—dressed in what became his trademark red jacket, and enthusiastically announced: "Good evening neighbors, and welcome to Musicarnival."

As Daykin recalled, when Price first met Wilbur in 1955, he was trying to decide whether to invest in the Hellman/Bernstein/Wilbur production of *Candide* or in another show that was in rehearsals at the time, *Damn Yankees,* the Jerry Ross and Richard Adler musical comedy starring Gwen Vernon, about a middle-aged man who sells his soul to the devil to become a crackerjack baseball player.

He decided on *Candide*, probably because it appealed to his intellect. As it turned out *Damn Yankees* ended up winning the 1956 Tony Award for Best Musical that year and ran for 1,019 performances in its original Broadway production with numerous Broadway revivals over the years.

Candide, on the other hand, opened in December 1956 at the Martin Beck Theatre on 45th Street (later in 2003 renamed the Al Hirschfeld Theatre) and closed after seventy-three performances— "a financial flop," Daykin said.

Despite his poor investment, Price was able to capitalize off *Damn Yankees* when he staged a production of the musical at his theater. A marketing genius, Price set his production in Cleveland, rather than Washington, D.C. as in the original, making the musical revolve around the Cleveland Indians instead of the Washington Senators. An experienced actor in his own right, Price also assumed the role of Van Buren in which he led his team of Cleveland Indians in a rousing rendition of the show-stopping song "Heart." And, for sure, when it came to Musicarnival, Price had "miles 'n miles n' miles of heart."

One Christmas season, Judith and John gave the Wilburs a very special Christmas present—a framed placard with his poem *Transit* that had appeared in subway cars and buses as part of New York City's Poetry in Motion program. Over the first twenty-five years of the program, which was founded in 1992, Poetry in Motion featured hundreds of poems from prominent American poets.

When *Transit* was the featured poem on a placard in 1994, Judith decided she had to have it! "Finally, I was on a train with only a few other passengers in my car," Judith said. So, with determination, she climbed up on the seat, no doubt shaking the whole time not only from the jerkiness of the train but from her own nervousness. She then snatched the placard out of its metal channels that held it in place. "The whole time I was trying to disappear into the wall of the car while pilfering this bit of Transit System memorabilia," Judith said.

Success! She sailed off the train at the next stop, perhaps a little sheepish, but placard firmly in hand. Later, Judith had the placard framed and that Christmas, she and John gave it to Dick and Charlee as a Christmas gift. "Dick was both amused and thrilled," Judith said. "And Charlee said it was one of her favorite poems."

LIFE IN KEY WEST during the winter months was laid back and leisurely. On Sunday, Charlee liked to go to the black Church of God of Prophesy on Elizabeth Street, just around the corner from the compound. It was a little church, one of the many historically black churches in Key West constructed originally in the late 1920s as a family dwelling.

"She liked the choir there," author Edward Hower said. "But she also liked to play the numbers and she knew a numbers-runner there."

Later in the afternoon Dick and Charlee might go for a bike ride around town. Like Hersey, they liked to ride their bicycles all over town, no doubt admiring Old Town's amazing architecture including the unique and ubiquitous gingerbread porches—porches with intricate hand-carved latticework—and de rigueur white picket fences.

Together, they would ride by and admire historic mansions, such as the twenty-two-room John Curry mansion on Caroline with its widow's walk, and the Greek revival houses, such as the one children's poet and illustrator Shel Silverstein owned at 618 William Street (which was heavily damaged during Hurricane Irma in 2017), and shotgun houses, arranged with one small room behind the other, and a long hallway from the front door to the back. (It was so-named supposedly because one could stand at the front door, shoot a gun, and the bullet would come out the back door.)

Or they might visit their neighbor poet James Merrill and

his partner David Jackson. The two had spent more than two decades writing the Ouija Board-inspired epic poem *The Changing Light at Sandover.* (It was published in three volumes between 1976 and 1980 and as one volume in 1982.) *Newsweek* magazine said the poem was most likely "...the greatest long poem, and at 560 pages, it is undoubtedly the longest great poem that an American yet produced."

After Merrill and Jackson's separation, Charlee introduced Merrill to Peter Hooten, an occasional actor, in 1983 with whom Merrill spent the next twelve years until his death in 1995.

Wilbur's writing schedule in Key West was rather haphazard. Unlike the rigorous daily writing schedule followed by his Key West friend and neighbor, John Hersey, Wilbur's schedule was less rigid. "I wish I could lay claim to habits," he once said. "I've always done a lot of working but not on a regular schedule. I never set apart a time of day to work. Sometimes I struggle for eight hours, sometimes I struggle for four hours, sometimes I don't write at all. Inspiration is an embarrassing word, but it's no good trying to write a poem if the words aren't coming to you . . . I sit down often and see what happens."

In the 1990s, Tom Taylor, who had been manager of the compound for many years passed away. What followed was a brief skirmish about who would become the new compound manager. Charles Lee wanted the job, but so did another longtime resident of the compound. As Lee said, "I remember telling Charlee one day, 'Well, I guess we'll have to bring it to a vote at our next annual meeting.'"

Charlee wouldn't hear of it. "Oh, no we won't," she said to Lee. "You're going to be the manager."

"And that, as they say, was that," Lee remembered. "She was literally the queen of the compound."

AS TRANQUIL AS LIFE WAS in the compound most of the time, there were, of course, occasional disputes or disagreements among the residents. One compound turmoil had to do with the Wilbur's beloved dog, a greyhound. "It was always amusing," said friend Ed Block, "to see Dick, who was quite a large man, walking down the street with this beautiful prancing dog by his side."

Not all the compound neighbors were thrilled about having the greyhound run around in the compound. As one compound resident said, "I don't remember the dog's name," (it was Durcie) "but I do remember how much it peed and crapped in our courtyard. They just let it run free until there was a flurry of complaints. So, they built an enclosed area beside their house and confined the dog there."

Around this time, there was a somewhat notorious greyhound racetrack on Stock Island, an island separated from Key West by Cow Key Channel. Known as the "Tiniest Track in America," the Key West Greyhound Track was literally, by all accounts, "the last stop on the road for young pups or aging greyhounds and the gullible tourists who bet on them."

At one point in its heyday, "buses left Duval Street every fifteen minutes to take the gamblers to the puppies." But in 1991, the health department shut down the track as the result of numerous health, safety, and fire code violations. As a result, the owners abandoned the business, leaving many of the malnourished dogs there to die.

By now, Durcie had died at age twelve, so Charlee and Dick tried to rescue a few of the greyhounds that had been abandoned at the racetrack. But soon afterwards, they came to a sad conclusion. As Dick said, the poor abused animals proved to be "too emotionally ruined" for them to take good care of.

THE CALL CAME ON THURSDAY MORNING, March 30, 1989, one month after Wilbur's sixty-eighth birthday. Wilbur had just returned home to the compound after a tennis match with noted publisher Ross Claiborne. The two, who were fairly evenly matched, played tennis frequently at the public courts in Bayview Park on Truman Avenue, just past White Street. Today, Wilbur won their three-set match, 6-4, 3-6, 6-4. But there was no doubt in either one's mind that Claiborne would just as likely walk away with the honor at their next match.

Walking into the tiny room he called his office in his equally tiny house in the compound, Wilbur answered the phone to learn—quite to his surprise—that he had won the Pulitzer Prize for Poetry—the second in his career, this one for his book *New and Collected Poems*.

It shouldn't have come as a surprise. After all, the reviews of the book had all been, without exception, effusive in their praise. Writing for the *New York Times*, Robert Richman, poetry editor of *The New Criterion*, said that the publication of the new book was "an occasion to celebrate. Mr. Wilbur's elegant verse reveals it is more than an Eden of beautiful language."

Still, it had been twelve years since the publication of his previous book, *The Mind-Reader: New Poems*, a reality Wilbur readily attributes to the fact that he is a "terribly slow" worker. (In 1989 he told a reporter he was working on a book of poems for children that he hoped would be "ready soon." Nine years later, in 1998, that delightful book, *The Disappearing Alphabet*, was finally published.)

Wilbur's response to his second Pulitzer was as humble as one might expect. "I'm astonished and pleased," he said. "I really wasn't expecting a thing."

Yet, as pleased as he was, he also must have realized that

prizes were not all that important. As he said after winning his first Pulitzer in 1957, "I don't think that prizes make a great difference to poets, if they're at all serious."

Charlee was equally pleased and gave her husband a big kiss. "That's a good start for a celebration," he told a Key West reporter.

BY 2005, CHARLEE HAD BEEN SICK for quite a while and was finding it more and more difficult to travel to Key West for the winter. So, after much discussion, they made the decision to leave Key West for good and return to Dodswell Road in Cummington, their home on eighty-plus acres that they had owned for more than forty years.

As they prepared to depart, Wilbur felt a bit sad as he reflected upon nearly three decades in this tropical paradise. "I'm going to miss Key West," he said, as the taxi pulled away to take them to the airport. "It's a place that makes me feel youthful."

In 2007, they sold their home in the compound, and asked their friend Billy Cauthen if he would bring a few possessions from the house up to them in Cummington. "All Dick really wanted," said Cauthen, "was his books." So, Cauthen dutifully packed up several boxes of books, and headed up north. On his way, he got word that Charlee had died.

A few days later, as the family gathered at the Cummington home, Billy had a Polaroid picture taken of Dick and him together. "When we looked at the picture," Cauthen said, "we saw an apparition, like a little snow ball, sitting on my shoulder."

"That's Charlee," Dick said. "She was waiting to see you."

For the next decade, until his death in 2017, Dick Wilbur

lived at his home in Cummington where he could be found puttering in his garden, tending to his basil and sage and roses, or welcoming his grandchildren for a visit whenever possible.

Of course, Wilbur could never leave the island he loved completely. From time to time, he would return to the island to visit friends or, as in 2010, to speak at the 28th Annual Key West Literary Seminar.

That year, the theme of the seminar focused on American poetry and the title of the four-day event— "Clearing the Sill of the World" —was taken from Wilbur's poem "The Writer."

The event was held at the San Carlos Theater in the beautiful historic building on Duval which served as a center for the Cuban community in the late 1800s. The San Carlos Institute was founded in 1871 by Cuban exiles of Key West as an educational, civic, and patriotic center. It was at the San Carlos that José Marti united the exile community in 1892 to launch the final phase of his campaign for Cuba's independence. Today, it serves as a museum, library, art gallery, theater, and school.

Several years later, Dick Wilbur, now in his nineties, was talking to a friend about his long life. Of his many accomplishments, he said there really was only one thing he hoped he would be remembered for. He said he would like to be remembered as a good and decent man.

And for those who knew Dick Wilbur, however casually, there was never any question.

Wilbur on Writing

"Writing involves lots of doubt, lots of groping around, waiting for a word that may not be there until next Tuesday."

~ **Richard Wilbur**

EPILOGUE

IT WAS A GLORIOUS DAY in the fall of 2018 when I returned to Key West and the Writers' Compound, after an almost seven-year absence. As I stood at the front gate to the compound, I thought about the four writers who lived there and the literary gifts they had given us all. I also thought about how they all respected the English language and the beauty (and power) of words, both singularly and in syntax, and the way words are formed to convey meaningful utterances in poetry and in prose. And I remembered a humorous poem (a clerihew) Wilbur had written for Ciardi's Festschrift*, *Measure of the Man*, about his insatiable consumption of words.

> When John Ciardi
>
> Is relaxing out in his yard, he
>
> Enlightens the flowers and birds
>
> Regarding the roots of words.

Hesitating at the wooden gate for a moment, nervous about what I might find inside (would it be as I had remembered?), I finally pushed open the gate that I had walked through so many times before.

Inside, I stopped and smiled. The lush, romantic, beautiful garden setting with exotic pink, yellow, and orange Bromeliads and peach hibiscus touched by an occasional zephyr told me I was home—home in a one-acre paradise on an island that Wallace Stevens had called a paradise nearly one hundred years earlier.

But, of course, there were changes. The two magnificent trees standing like noble sentries on either side of the gate to the compound were gone, thanks to Hurricane Irma in 2017. My friend and landlord in the orange Crocs had passed away, as had Richard Wilbur, the last of the four writers in the original Writers' Compound on Windsor.

OFF AND ON FOR THE PAST SEVEN YEARS, I had read about, talked about, researched, and figuratively lived with these four American writers from the compound. In the process, they became part of me, part of my soul. In my journey into the past, I laughed with Ellison at the thought of bean-pods beating down on his roof; I listened to Ciardi pontificate in his Hawaiian shirt as he "held court" at the small swimming pool in the compound; I rode my bike alongside Wilbur as we both admired the unique gingerbread architecture of Key West; and I vicariously joined in a rousing game of anagrams with the whole group, who'll never know that I just added one letter to the word SHANK—a word Hersey would know is more than just a cut of beef, but the part of a fishhook between the eye and the bend—and rearranged the letters to make THANKS— thanks to these four American writers for the amazing journey they took me on.

Throughout my journey into the past, I had asked many writers, publishers, and others what drew them to Key West. I got many answers: "It was the end of the road"; "it was the warm, tropical environment"; "it was the freedom and acceptance of everyone, by everyone."

But there is one writer who best summed up the beauty of Key West and the answer to the question about what has always drawn so many writers to it. Jefferson B. Browne, who wrote a definitive history of Key West from 1815 to

1912 nearly a century ago, expressed his love for the island this way.

"Come weal, come woe; come progress, come decay;

Come nature with her beauty; come man with his mistakes;

Nothing can mar the sky, the water, the sunrise and the sunset,

Which make the unchanging and unchangeable Key West!"

Jefferson B. Browne, 1912

Festschrift: [from German: fest: feast; festival + Schrift: writing] a volume of articles, essays, etc. contributed by many authors in honor of a colleague, usually published on the occasion of retirement or important anniversary. In the end, the Festschrift on Ciardi became a memorial volume, *John Ciardi, Measure of the Man* (Fayetteville, AR: The University of Arkansas Press, 1987).

Appendix 1: Key West Authors

In addition to the four authors who are the subjects of this book, other Key West writers mentioned in the text include:

Philip Burton (1904 – 1995): Angela Street; writer, teacher, director.

Judy Blume (1938 -): Flagler Street; author of juvenile and young adult fiction.

John Malcolm Brinnin (1916 – 1998): Truman Annex; poet, literary critic.

John Dos Passos (1896 - 1970): 1401 Pine Street; novelist.

Robert Frost (1874 - 1963): Caroline Street; poet (winner of four Pulitzer Prizes for Poetry).

James Leo Herlihy (1927 - 1993): 709 Baker's Lane; author.

Edward Hower: 1313 Reynolds; novelist.

David A. Kaufelt (1939 - 2014): Flagler Street; novelist, founder of the Key West Literary Seminar.

Lynn Mitsuko Kaufelt: Flagler Street; cofounder, Key West Literary Seminar; author, *Key West Writers and Their Houses*.

James (Jimmie) Kirkwood (1924 - 1989): Catherine Street; novelist, playwright, winner of the 1976 Pulitzer Prize for Drama (*A Chorus Line*).

Alison Lurie (1926 -): 1313 Reynolds; novelist, Pulitzer Prize winner (*Foreign Affairs*).

Thomas McGuane (1939 -): Love Lane, 123-125 Ann Street, 1011 Von Phister Street, 416 Elizabeth; novelist.

Terrance McNally (1938 -   ):   Playwright, librettist, and screenwriter.

James Merrill (1926 - 1995): 702 Elizabeth; poet, Pulitzer Prize for Poetry (*Divine Comedies*).

Shel Silverstein (1930 - 1999): 620 William Street; author of children's books.

Tennessee Williams (1911 - 1983): 1431 Duncan Street; playwright.

Appendix II: Chronology

1914: Ellison is born (March 1)

1914: Hersey is born (June 17)

1916: Ciardi is born (June 24)

1921: Wilbur is born (March 1)

1940: Ciardi's first book of poems, *Homeward to America*, is published.

1942: Wilbur marries Charlotte (Charlee) Hayes Ward.

1945: Hersey wins Pulitzer Prize for *A Bell for Adano*; published in 1944.

1946: Ellison marries second wife, Fanny McConnell.

1946: Ciardi marries Myra Judith Hostetter (known as Judith).

1947: Wilbur publishes his first book, *The Beautiful Changes and Other Poems*.

1952: Ellison publishes *Invisible Man*.

1953: Ellison wins the National Book Award

1957: Wilbur wins Pulitzer Prize for Poetry for *Things of This World*.

1958: Hersey marries second wife, Barbara Day Addams Kaufman

1967: House fire destroys part of manuscript of Ellison's second novel.

1976: The writers buy homes in the Windsor Lane compound (March).

> Ciardi, age 60
>
> Hersey, age 61
>
> Ellison, age 62
>
> Wilbur, age, 55

1986: Ciardi dies (age 69) of heart attack on Easter Sunday, Metuchen, NJ.

1987: Wilbur is appointed Poet Laureate of the United States.

1989: Wilbur wins second Pulitzer Prize for *New and Collected Poems.*

1993: Hersey dies at Key West home (age 78).

1994: Ellison dies of pancreatic cancer in Manhattan (age 80).

2017: Wilbur dies, Belmont, Massachusetts (age 96).

Appendix III: Key West Literary Landmarks

Date Dedicated	Name	Location
1993	Elizabeth Bishop's Key West House	624 White Street
1994	Harry S. Truman Little White House	111 Front Street
1994	San Carlos Institute-José Marti	516 Duval Street
1995	John Hersey's Key West House	719F Windsor Lane
1995	Robert Frost's Key West Cottage	410 Caroline Street
1996	Wallace Stevens/Casa Marina Hotel	1500 Reynolds St.
2004	Tennessee Williams' Key West House	1431 Duncan St.
2010	Ernest Hemingway Home & Museum	907 Whitehead St.
2016	Key West Pubic Library/David Kaufelt	1025 Fleming Street

All direct quotes attributed to the following individuals are from personal interviews on the dates indicated.

Ed Block: December 14, 2011   Edward Hower: January 20, 2012

Billy Cauthen: December 20, 2011   Charles Lee: January 10, 2012

Ross Claiborne: November 15, 2011   Alison Lurie: January 20, 2012

Judith Daykin: November 10, 2011   Dick Reynolds: November 2, 2011

Tom Wilson: December 20, 2011

Note: RWEP, LC refers to Ralph Waldo Ellison Papers, Library of Congress.

Prologue

"all the fascinating and crazy people": James Kirkwood cited in Betty Williams, "Kirkwood enjoys time off in Key West," *Key West Citizen*, January 6, 1985.

"Where the narrative strays": John Berendt, *Midnight in the Garden of Good and Evil* (New York: Random House, 1994).

"The general tenet": Lee Gutman, *You Can't Make This Stuff Up* (New York: Da Capo Press, 2012).

"Writing non-fiction is a lot harder": Alison Lurie.

Introduction

"The soul of Key West": Liner notes, Jimmy Buffett, *Barometer Soup* (released August 1995).

"mysterious, funky, and indescribably exotic": James Leo Herlihy cited in Lynn Mitsuko Kaufelt, *Key West Writers and Their Houses* (Sarasota, Fl: Pineapple Press, 1986).

"world wanderers from every portion of the globe": Jefferson B. Browne, *Key West: The Old and the New* (St. Augustine, FL: The Record

Company Printers and Publishers, 1912), p. 174.

"in consideration of several": Jefferson B. Browne, *Key West: The Old and the New.*

"Capital and capitalists will always go": Jefferson B. Browne, *Key West: The Old and the New,* Appendix J: Memorial to Congress (St. Augustine, FL: The Record Company Printers and Publishers, 1912), p. 209.

"dream fulfilled": Cheryl Blackberry, "Flagler-built Casa Marina has rich past, magical moments," *Palm Beach Daily News*, January 24, 2015.

"It was very much like": Wallace Stevens cited in Dariel Suarez, "A Poet's Escape: The Key West Idyll (and Turmoil) of Wallace Stevens," *The Florida Book Review,* n.d. www.floridabookreview.net/wallace-stevens.html

"he was fed up with": Wendy Tucker, Betty Williams, Maureen Delaney, "Agents arrest 13 here on federal indictments for drug trafficking and other charges," *Key West Citizen*, June 29, 1984.

"drug smugglers thrived and cocaine": Liz Lear, "Thomas McGuane, 1984," Key West Literary Seminar. https://www.kwls.org/key-wests-life-of-letters/thomas_mcguane_1984_the_liz_le/

"Key West was wide open": Billy Cauthen.

"a sleepy, wartime hangover": Michael Adano, "This Man *Is* an Island," *The Bitter Southerner,* n.d. http://bittersoutherner.com/this-man-is-an-island-david-wolkowsky-key-west/

"Not so much the honky-tonk tourist side": Amy Driscoll, "He's Mr. Key West – and owner of his own private island," *The Miami Herald,* August 4, 2012. https://www.miamiherald.com/latest-news/article1941790.html

"He's Mr. Key West,": Judy Blume as cited in Amy Driscoll, "He's Mr. Key West."

"precisely twelve and a half": J. Wills Burke, *The Streets of Key West: A History Through Street Names* (Sarasota, FL: Pineapple Press, October 2015).

"It had become a hippie hang-out": Judith Daykin.

"dry out his bones": J. Willis Burke, *The Streets of Key West: A History Through Street Names* (Sarasota, Fl: Pineapple Press, 2014).

"infinitely superior to the usual guidebook": Richard Wilbur cited in Betty Williams, "Novice's book raises Conch eyebrows," *Key West Citizen,* February 27, 1983.

"Key West was always a very tolerant": Alison Lurie.

"The book was well received": Alison Lurie cited in Betty Williams, "Lurie joins Pulitzer set," *Key West Citizen,* April 28, 1985.

"At a party here": Lynn Kaufelt cited in "In Winter, U.S. Writing Talent Pools on the Sensual, Timeless Port of Key West," *People* magazine, February 23, 1981.

"I love the fact": Ross Claiborne.

"schmoozing over Diet Cokes": David Kaufelt, Key West Literary Seminar program, 1990. https://www.kwls.org/lit/kwls_blog/among_the_archives/index.cfm

"Key West is no longer": Wallace Stevens cited in "The Trouble with Robert Frost and Wallace Stevens," *Life in Letters,* The Key West Literary Seminar. https://www.kwls.org/key-wests-life-of-letters/post_11/

"if someone had dropped you down": James Kirkwood cited in Betty Williams, "Kirkwood enjoys time off in Key West," *Key West Citizen*, January 6, 1985.

"began to glamorize it": Richard Wilbur, "Discovering Key West," Web of Stories. https://webofstories.com/play/richard.wilbur/37

"Freud said that we are at our most creative": David Kaufelt, *Key West's Life of Letters,* Key West Literary Seminar. https://www.kwls.org/key-wests-life-of-letters/david-a-kaufelt-1939-2014/

"You can have the rest": Jimmy Buffett, "I Have Found Me a Home," *A White Sport Coat and a Pink Crustacean*, 1973.

"I wanted to reclaim": "J.T. Thompson: The Human Behind 'One Human Family,'" *Florida Keys News*, January 6, 2017. https://fla-keys.com/news/article/9432/

Chapter 1: John Ciardi

"A combination of a Hemingway": Norman Cousins cited in Jeff Lovill *John Ciardi: Measure of the Man*, (Fayetteville, AR: University of Arkansas Press, 1987), p. 61.

"The essential kindness of the man": Vince Clemente cited in *John Ciardi: Measure of the Man,* p. 129.

"sun-drenched breakfasts on the patio": Edward M. Cifelli, ed., *The Selected Letters of John Ciardi* (Fayetteville, AR: University of Arkansas Press, 1991) p. 293.

"I'm ready to sit in Florida": Ibid, p. 285.

"I am in a green paradise,": Ibid, p. 327.

"brash young man.": Vince Clemente, *Measure of the Man*, p. 16.

"dutifully watched out for me": Ibid, p. 16.

"You couldn't help but feel": Judith Daykin.

"Often there stands a wife," Edna Healey, *Wives of Fame* (London, England: Sidgwick & Jackson Ltd., 1986).

"Because Ciardi was so big and noisy": Alison Lurie.

tasted like jet fuel: Vince Clemente, *Measure of the Man*, p. 62

"I don't know how I": John Ciardi cited in *Key West Citizen*, March 15, 1981.

"appealed only to the adolescent mind": Edward M. Cifellli, *John Ciardi: A Biography* (Fayetteville, AR: The University of Arkansas Press, 1997), p. 152.

"What he knew about": John Ciardi, *Manner of Speaking* (New Brunswick, NJ: Rutgers University Press, 1972), p. 63.

"I had no idea": Vince Clemente, *Measure of the Man,* p. 9.

"He would invent": Solares Hill, May 1986.

"They would take turns": Benn Ciardi cited in Jay Bodas, "'Lucky John's' love of poetry led to full life," *Sentinel-EBS News,* June 9, 2005. https://www1.gmnews.com/2005/06/page/101/

"I love the work obsessively": Edward M. Cifelli, ed., *The Selected Letters of John Ciardi,* p 321.

"Being fascinated by words": John Ciardi cited in "Poet-author visits KWHS," *Key West Citizen*, February 13, 1983.

"fashionable to consider John Ciardi": Vincent Clemente, *Measure of the Man*, p. 192.

"smug and self-important": David Wojahn, *Poetry* magazine, June 1985, pp. 169-170.

"come close to being greeting card verse.": Edward M. Cifelli, ed., *The Selected Letters of John Ciardi,* p. 459.

"Some of the best everywhere": On card to Monroe Public Library, July 14, 1981**"I have stopped:"** Ciefelli, p. 458.

"The piece was decidedly": David Wojahn to author, e-mail, December 20, 2011.

"I am left with a sense": Letter to James I. Armstrong, President of Middlebury College, administrators of the Bread Loaf conference,

August 1972.

"I ask that there be no": Edward M. Cifelli, ed., *The Selected Letters of John Ciardi*, p. 268.

"mostly because there isn't time": Edward M. Cifelli, ed., *The Selected Letters of John Ciardi,* p. 454.

"I used to smoke and drink": John Ciardi cited in William Green, *Arkansas Gazette*, Oct 20, 1981.

"I think son Jonnel": Edward M. Cifelli, ed., *The Selected Letters of John Ciardi,* p. 397.

"I got a royalty statement": Ibid, p. 333.

"There is nothing wrong": A-Z Quotes. John Ciardi. https://www.azquotes.com/author/2891-John_Ciardi.

"Ciardi was a show-off": Edward Hower.

"Everyone pretty much got along": Tom Wilson.

"You bought your house": Charles Lee.

"Each was flexing": Dick Reynolds.

"Of course, I used to play him,": Bach Cantatas Website: Lazar Berman (Piano). www.bach-cantatas.com/Bio/Berman-Lazar.htm.

"John always had to have an audience": Philip Burton cited in Solares Hill, May 1986.

"I never much respected it": Edward M. Cifelli, ed., *The Selected Letters of John Ciardi,* p. 409.

"He is a beautiful gent": Edward M. Cifelli, ed., *The Selected Letters of John Ciardi* Selected, p. 397.

"Mrs. Lindbergh has written": John Ciardi, *Dialogue with an Audience* (New York: J. B. Lippincott Company, 1963), p. 77.

Post Mortem: Seven years later: Eric Pace, "Gibson Danes, Dean, 81, and Ilse Getz, Artist, 75," *The New York Times*, 1992.

"I call it a pain": Edward M. Cifelli, ed., *The Selected Letters of John Ciardi,* p. 446.

"The actuarial tables": Vince Clemente, *Measure of the Man*, p.19.

"benign, cozy, sleepy": Richard Wilbur cited in George Fontana, "Pulitzer winners acknowledge Bishop's influence on them," *Key West Citizen*, January 11, 1993.

He would have been most pleased: "Poet John Ciardi, acclaimed for

Translation of 'Inferno' Dies," Associated Press, The Los Angeles Times, April 1, 1986. http://articles.latimes.com/1986-04-01/news/mn-1539_1_john-ciardi

"the language of experience": John Ciardi, Miller Williams, *How Does a Poem Mean?* (New York: Houghton Mifflin, 1975).

Chapter 2: Ralph Ellison

"Ellison's outlook was universal": Anne Seidlitz, American Masters, NPR http://www.pbs.org/wnet/americanmasters/ralph-ellison-an-american-journey/587/

"I wanted the world": Ralph Ellison cited in "That Same Pain, That Same Pleasure: An Interview," in *The Collected Essays of Ralph Ellison*, ed. John F. Callahan (New York: Modern Library Classics), 2003, p. 65.

"young Renaissance Men": Ralph Ellison, *Shadow and Act* (New York: Random House, 1964).

"more or less a slob. He always": Alison Lurie.

"Why do you always hire": Charles Lee.

"Key West city directories": Jerry Wilkinson, "Black History," keys history.org. http://www.keyshistory.org/blackhistory.html

"dilapidated compound": Ralph Ellison to Mrs. Charles Etta Tucker, letter, April 12, 1985, RWEP, LC.

"The Ellisons were almost": Tom Wilson.

"The grounds which we share": Ralph Ellison to Mrs. Charles Etta Tucker, letter, April 12, 1985, RWEP, LC.

"explode button-shaped seeds": Ibid.

"new writers could be or should be": Charles Norman cited in David Haward Bain, *Whose Woods These Are: A History of the Bread Loaf Writers' Conference 1926-1992* (Hopewell, NJ: Ecco Press, 1993), p. 16.

"A sense of easy intimacy": Arnold Rampersad, *Ralph Ellison: A Biography* (New York: Alfred A. Knopf, 2007).

"many beautiful things": Fanny Ellison to Rose Styron, letter, October 17, 1967, RWEP, LC.

"with the enthusiasm": IBID

"interesting enough and humorous enough": Ralph Ellison to "Charlie," letter, August 10, 1968, Ralph Waldo Ellison Papers, Library of Congress.

"Usually, it's black tie": Ibid.

Fanny, however, never did totally buy: Hinton Als, "In the Territory: A

Look at the Life of Ralph Ellison," *The New Yorker,* May 7, 2007.

"a full copy of all that he had done": Arnold Rampersad, *Ralph Ellison: A Biography.*

Still, later, he claimed: Ralph Ellison to David Remnick, "Visible Man," *The New Yorker,* March 14, 1994.

"sheer devastation of what": Ralph Ellison to "Charlie," letter, August 10, 1968.

"there will be something": David Remnick, "Visible Man."

"I came to suspect": Jervis Anderson, "Ralph Ellison Goes Home," *The New Yorker,* November 22, 1976.

"A metamorphosis from": Ralph Ellison, *Going to the Territory* (New York: Vintage Books, a division of Random House, 1986).

"Richard Wright took me": Ralph Ellison cited in John Hersey, ed., *Ralph Ellison: A Collection of Critical Essays* (Englewood Cliffs, N.J.: Prentice Hall, 1974).

"I approached writing": Ibid.

"sharp tongue": Jervis Anderson, "Ralph Ellison Goes Home."

"Taylor had a reputation": Ross Claiborne.

"Instead, I resented": Ralph Ellison to Richard Wilbur, letter, February 25, 1987, Ralph Waldo Ellison Papers, Library of Congress.

"as long as they didn't make it obvious.": Arnold Rampersad, *Ralph Ellison: A Biography.*

"to Marilyn, the Taylors were by far the liveliest": Fred Lawrence Guiles, *Norma Jean: The Life and Death of Marilyn Monroe* (New York: Harper Collins, 1985).

"threatened with blacklisting": Ibid.

"It's not that it's needed": Stephen Morris cited in Chris Doyle, "Gays march in solidarity," *Key West Citizen,* June 21, 1993.

"presumably they could have occupied": Ralph Ellison to Richard Wilbur, letter, February 25, 1987.

"a violation of friendship": Ibid.

"being square, and holding": Ibid.

"assumed they were phoning": Ibid.

"dirtied by Frank Taylor and his lover." Arnold Rampersad, *Ralph Ellison: A Biography.*

"the cruel Ellisons": Ralph Ellison to Richard Wilbur, letter, Feb 25, 1987.

"...to ascribe the break in friendship": Ralph Ellison to Richard Wilbur, letter, February 24, 1987.

"the fun we had together": Charlee Wilbur to Fanny Ellison and RWE, letter, February 15, 1987, RWEP, LC.

"And everyone seems to be aware": Ibid.

"When you spent a year abroad": Ralph Ellison to Richard Wilbur, letter, February 24, 1987.

"The fact that other friends": Ibid.

"I hope this gives you a clearer idea": Ibid.

"I am terribly stubborn": Ralph Ellison cited in *Ralph Ellison: A Collection of Critical Essays*.

Chapter 3: John Hersey

"To be in his presence": Anthony Lewis, columnist, *The New York Times,* The Writers' Compound as cited in *Yale Alumni* Magazine, October 1993. http://archives.yalealumnimagazine.com/issues/93_10/hersey.html

"Of all the artists I've known": Richard Wilbur cited in Andy Newman, "John Hersey home dedicated as U.S. literary landmark," *The Key West Citizen*, January 16, 1995.

"He was very shy": Barbara Hersey cited in Andy Newman, "John Hersey home dedicated as U.S. literary landmark."

"With Hersey you could go": Ed Block.

"down in the mouth and limp": Peter Feibleman cited in "A Life in Writing: John Hersey, 1914-1993," Yale Alumni Magazine, October 1993. http://archives.yalealumnimagazine.com/issues/93_10/hersey.html

"He was a New England-bred": Dick Reynolds.

"Hersey could be very formal": Alison Lurie.

"an Italian-American major": Book description, Amazon.com.

"afforded a spectacular view": Jonathan Dee, "John Hersey, The Art of Fiction No. 92," *The Paris Review*, Issue 100, Summer-Fall 1986.

"He was very regular in his habits": Baird Hersey cited in Russell Shorto, "John Hersey, the Writers Who Let 'Hiroshima' Speak for Itself," *The New Yorker*, August 31, 2016. https://www.newyorker.com/culture/culture-desk/john-hersey-the-writer-who-let-hiroshima-speak-for-itself

"You could set your watch": Judith Daykin.

"the ties between": *The New Yorker* review as cited in Editorial Reviews, *Blues*, amazon.com.

"If no creature is mortal": John Ciardi, "The Lung Fish," *For Instance* (New York: W.W. Norton & Company, 1979), p. 54.

"with a glaze made": Daniel Mueller, "The Middle Ground," *The Iowa Review*, May 4, 2017. http://uiowa.3dcartstores.com/Spring-2017-Vol-47-Iss-1_p_80.html

"We should have read": Charles Lee.

"Barbara was a beautiful lady": Billy Cauthen.

"You had the sense it": Tom Wilson.

"socially acceptable mayhem.": *The Miami Herald*, Jan 24, 1994. Miami Herald.

"knew all the names of all the fish": Arlo Haskell, "The World Is Fundamentally a Great Wonder: A Conversation with Richard Wilbur," Key West Literary Seminar, 10/21/2009, updated on 10/16/2017. https://www.kwls.org/key-wests-life-of-letters/the_world_is_fundamentally_a_g/

"massive, pyknic build": Brook Hersey, John Hersey Memorial program.

"three dictionaries": John Hersey, "A Game of Anagrams," *Key West Tales* (New York: Random House, date), p. 109.

"takes his time transforming the dread": Ibid., p. 117.

"We didn't play much": John Malcolm Brinnin cited in *Key West Citizen*, January 24, 1994.

"appropriating another writer's facts": Elizabeth Mehren, "John Hersey's New Yorker Mea Culpa," *Los Angeles Times,* July 28, 1988. http://articles.latimes.com/keyword/john-hersey

"I don't believe my real offense": "John Hersey Apologizes for Lifting Facts and Phrases," Associated Press, Los Angeles Times, July 22, 1988. http://articles.latimes.com/1988-07-22/news/mn-7740_1_john-hersey

"This sounded nothing like": Steven Mufson, *Washington Post,* March 25, 1993.

"no Talk of the Town, no cartoons, no reviews": Joshua Rothman, "John Hersey's Hiroshima," *The New Yorker*, August 6, 2015. https://www.newyorker.com/books/double-take/john-herseys-hiroshima-now-online

"Hersey's reporting was so meticulous": Hendrick Hertzberg, "John Hersey," *The New Yorker*, April 5, 1993.

https://www.newyorker.com/magazine/1993/04/05/john-hersey

"Our teacher, who was the only": Edward Hower to author, interview, January 20, 2012.

"He was the type of person": Brook Hersey, John Hersey Memorial Program.

"If I weren't writing a book": John Hersey cited in *The Miami Herald*, March 25, 1993.

"I have five kids": John Hersey Cited in *Key West Citizen*, March 22, 1981.

"at the tiny white-fenced cemetery": Daniel Mueller, "The Middle Ground."

"It was an occasion of celebration," David Wolkowsky cited in Vernon Silver, "Hersey Remembered by his Friends," *Key West Citizen*, June 23, 1993.

"I remember thinking:" Peter Feibleman cited in "A Life in Writing: John Hersey, 1914-1993."

In dying, he wanted: Brook Hersey, John Hersey Memorial program.

Hersey on Writing: John Hersey cited in "31 Notable Quotes by John Hersey on Journalism, Learning, Failure, and More."
https://quotes.thefamouspeople.com/john-hersey-4890.php

Chapter 4: Richard Wilbur

"Courtly, courteous, and civilized": Sam Gwynn cited in Cynthia Haven, "Touching the Good," *The Book Haven* blog," Stanford University, November 7, 2017.

"Why do you take winter vacations": Richard Wilbur, "Discovering Key West," *Web of Stories*, ca. 2005, www.webofstories.com.

"I remember when we settled in": Richard Wilbur to Arlo Haskell, interview, "The World is Fundamentally a Great Wonder: A Conversation with Richard Wilbur," Key West Literary Seminar, October 21, 2009.

"The great thing about Key West": Richard Wilbur, "Discovering Key West."

"In those days": Richard Wilbur, "Finding the Right Girl for Me," *Web of Stories*, ca. 2005, www.webofstories.com.

"the first friend of my poetry": Robert Frost cited in "Robert Frost," *Web of Stories*, ca 2005, www.webofstories.com.

"I was absolutely addled": Jeffrey Cramer, "Long love and constant spirits: an interview with Richard and Charlee Wilbur," *The Literary Review*, June 22, 2002. http://www.highbeam.com/doc/1G1-91040703.html

"I felt happy": Ibid.

"the perfect poet's wife": Ibid.

"Charlee was the driving force": Charles Lee.

"Charlee, without being": Jeffrey Cramer, "Long love and constant spirits: an interview with Richard and Charlee Wilbur."

"You're a dolt!": Charlee Wilbur cited in Robert Bagg and Mary Bagg, *Let Us Watch Richard Wilbur: A Biographical Study* (Amherst, MA: University of Massachusetts Press, 2017).

"I was terribly lucky": Richard Wilbur, "Finding the Right Girl for Me."

"When I don't have notions": Vicki Sanders, "2 Captured by Poetry," *The Miami Herald*, March 11, 198**"I almost always have"**: Arlo Haskell, "The World Is Fundamentally a Great Wonder: A Conversation with Richard Wilbur."

"We were always being told": Charlee Wilbur cited in David H. van Biema, "Richard Wilbur," *People* magazine, October 5, 1987.

"Charlee was a very strong, independent": Dick Reynolds.

"freelance counselor in genetic": Vicki Sanders, "2 Captured by Poetry," *Miami Herald*, March 11, 1984.

"capable of keeping a checkbook": David H. van Biema, "Richard Wilbur," *People* magazine, October 5, 1987.)

"We were suddenly climbing": Sunil Iyengar, "Richard Wilbur: A Conversation." http://www.cprw.com/Iyengar/wilbur.htm

"I had the luck to be": Ibid.

"I didn't know who": Billy Cauthen.

"But after he signed it": Tom Wilson.

"I'm waiting and waiting and waiting": Judith Daykin.

"chorus girls breaking into routines": John E. Vacha, *The Music Went 'Round and Around: The Story of Musicarnival* (Kent, OH: Kent State University Press, 2014). https://www.goodspeed.org/My%20Files/Musicarnival.pdf

"miles 'n miles 'n miles of heart": From *Damn Yankees*, lyrics by Jerry Ross.

"She liked the choir there," Edward Hower.

"the greatest long poem": *Newsweek magazine,* cited in Editorial Reviews, *The Changing Light at Sandover*, Kindle Edition, amazon.com.

"I wish I could lay claim": Vicki Sanders, "2 Captured by Poetry," *The Miami Herald*, March 11, 1984.

"It was always amusing": Ed Block.

"I don't remember the dog's name": Compound resident to author.

"the last stop on the road": Mark Syverud, "Syverud: There's more than one way to beat the odds," The Daily Messenger, July 8, 2016.

"buses left Duval street": Dave Joseph, "It's Going to the Dogs": *Sun—Sentinel*, April 22, 1990. http://articles.sun-sentinel.com/1990-04-22/sports/9001040421_1_mallory-square-dogs-greyhound/2

"too emotionally ruined": Edward Steinhardt, "From Dodwells Road: Friends, Frost, & the Love Lost." Richard Wilbur, August 12, 2010. http://readingaboutrichardwilbur.blogspot.com

"an occasion to celebrate. Mr. Wilbur's elegant verse": Robert Richman, "Benevolent Possessions." 1988. http://www.nytimes.com/1988/05/29/books/benevolent-possessions.html

"I'm astonished and pleased": "Proud of Richard Wilbur," *Key West Citizen*, April 2, 1989.

"I don't think prizes": Richard Wilbur in "Candide Comes to Broadway," Web of Stories.

"That's a good start": Richard Wilbur cited in "City Poet wins Pulitzer," March 31, 1989.

"I'm going to miss Key West": Richard Wilbur cited in Edward Steinhardt, "From Dodwells Road: Friends, Frost, & the Love Lost

"Writing involves:" Richard Wilbur cited in Elizabeth Kastor, "The Lyricist as Laureate: Poet Richard Wilbur Reflect on His New Post," *The Washington Post,* October 6, 1987.

Epilogue

"When John Ciardi:" Richard Wilbur cited in *Measure of the Man."*

"Come weal, come woe": Jefferson, B. Browne, *Key West: The Old and the New.*

BIBLIOGRAPHY

Bagg, Robert and Mary Bragg. *Let Us Watch Richard Wilbur: A Biographical Study.* Amherst, MA: University of Massachusetts Press, 2017.

Bain, David Haward. *Whose Woods These Are: A History of the Bread Loaf Writers' Conference 1926-1992.* Hopewell, NJ: Ecco Press, 1993.

Browne, Jefferson B. *Key West: The Old and the New.* St. Augustine, FL: The Record Company Printers and Publishers, 1912.

Burke, J. Wills. *The Streets of Key West: A History Through Street Names.* Sarasota, FL: Pineapple Press, October 2015.

Ciardi, John. *Dialogue with an Audience.* New York: J. B. Lippincott Company, 1963.

_____. *For Instance.* New York: W.W. Norton & Company, 1979.

_____. *Manner of Speaking.* New Brunswick, NJ: Rutgers University Press, 1972.

Cifelli, Edward M. *John Ciardi: A Biography.* Fayetteville, AR: The University of Arkansas Press, 1997.

_____, ed. *The Selected Letters of John Ciardi.* Fayetteville, AR: University of Arkansas Press, 1991.

Clemente, Vincent, ed. *John Ciardi: Measure of the Man.* Fayetteville, AR: University of Arkansas Press, 1987.

Cox, Christopher. *A Key West Companion.* New York, NY: St. Martin's Press, 1983.

Ellison, Ralph. *Going to the Territory.* New York: Vintage Books, a division of Random House, 1986.

_____, *Shadow and Act.* New York: Random House, 1964.

Guilds, Fred Lawrence. *Norma Jean: The Life and Death of Marilyn Monroe.* New York: Harper Collins, 1985.

Healey, Edna. *Wives of Fame.* London: Bloomsbury Reader, 2011.

Hersey, John. *Key West Tales.* New York: Random House.

_____, ed. *Ralph Ellison: A Collection of Critical Essays.* Englewood Cliffs, N.J.: Prentice Hall, January 1974.

Kaufelt, Lynn Mitsuko. *Key West Writers and Their Houses.* Sarasota, Fl: Pineapple Press, 1986.

Ogle, Maureen. *Key West: History of an Island of Dreams.* Gainesville, FL: University Press of Florida, 2006.

Rampersand, Arnold. *Ralph Ellison: A Biography.* New York: Alfred A. Knopf, 2007.

Vacha, John E. *The Music Went 'Round and Around: The Story of Musicarnival.* Kent: Ohio: The Kent State University Press, 2004.

ABOUT THE AUTHOR

Jack L. Roberts is the author of more than two dozen nonfiction books for young readers (mostly biographies), published by some of the foremost educational publishing companies in the country, including Lerner Books, Benchmark Education, Teacher Created Materials, and Scholastic Inc. Mr. Roberts began his career in educational publishing at Children's Television Workshop (now Sesame Workshop) where he was senior editor for the *Sesame Street/Electric Company* Reading Kits. Later, he launched several magazines at Scholastic Inc. for middle school students as well as for teachers and administrators. In 2007, he co-founded *WordTeasers*, an educational series of games designed to help young people improve their vocabulary through "conversation rather than memorization." In 2017 he launched Curious Kids Press (curiouskidspress.com), an educational book publishing company, focusing primarily, though not exclusively, on nonfiction books for young readers about countries and cultures around the world. The company has published two series of country-specific books— "A Kid's Guide to..." for ages 9-12 and "Let's Visit" for ages 6-8. This is his first trade nonfiction for adults.

Made in the USA
Columbia, SC
08 June 2023

17751357R00085